Efficiency Best Practices for Microsoft 365

Discover ways to improve your efficiency and save time using M365 applications

Dr. Nitin Paranjape

BIRMINGHAM—MUMBAI

Efficiency Best Practices for Microsoft 365

Group Product Manager: Pavan Ramchandani
Publishing Product Manager: Aaron Tanna
Senior Editor: Keagan Carneiro
Content Development Editor: Adrija Mitra
Technical Editor: Joseph Aloocaran
Copy Editor: Safis Editing
Project Coordinator: Manthan Patel
Proofreader: Safis Editing
Indexer: Sejal Dsilva
Production Designer: Jyoti Chauhan

First published: December 2021

Production reference: 1191121

Published by Packt Publishing Ltd.
Livery Place
35 Livery Street
Birmingham
B3 2PB, UK.

978-1-80107-226-7

www.packt.com

*To Dr. Nandini and Zeus Paranjape, and the billions of people
who use Microsoft Office across the globe.*

Dear Andy Glover

Learn & Grow

nsgujape

Contributors

About the author

Dr. Nitin Paranjape (Doc) completed his post-graduation in medicine – obstetrics and gynecology (he did complete it!) – in Mumbai, India. Technology was his hobby. Initially, he developed many medical applications, first on the Sinclair Spectrum and then on PCs. Soon he expanded to corporate IT.

His organization (Mediline) was one of the earliest partners of Microsoft in India. For 15 years, he was considered to be the pioneer of the entire Microsoft platform, cutting across programming tools, databases, infrastructure, and Office. However, he noticed that most of the technologies were largely underutilized – due to which people were still inefficient.

Therefore, he changed his focus to the most commonly used (and most underused) tool in the world – Microsoft Office. Now, he is known as the Productivity Guru and Dr. Productivity.

He has coached over 400,000 professionals across 3,000+ customers in 18 countries. He even coaches Microsoft's own staff and partners about the effective utilization of the Microsoft 365 platform. Having authored 700+ articles in print and 1,000+ blogs, he is a prolific writer, a sought-after orator, and an accomplished speaker.

He uses a simple, down-to-earth, humorous storytelling style enhanced with live demos to educate and empower his audience. Customers call his sessions a "magic show!".

He is also a PROSCI-certified change management consultant.

Doc's passion is to improve the efficiency of every user of the Office platform.

This book is the distillation of his knowledge and experience gained over 30 years of work.

First of all, I want to thank Raj Chaudhuri, my close friend and a genius technologist, who pushed me to write the book.

I was also privileged to have Vesa Nopanen, Chantal Bossé, and Raj Chaudhuri as content reviewers. I thank them for their invaluable input, suggestions, and details, which have enhanced the content significantly.

I also want to thank Shesham Patil, who helped me during the entire process of writing, publishing, and marketing the book. Thanks to Zeus, my son, for being my constant sounding board throughout the writing process.

Special thanks to Valentine Dsouza and Meena Nair, for refining the language and content of the book.

Finally, a big thank you to the professional publishing team at Packt: Adrija Mitra, Keagan Carnerio, Aaron Tanna, Divij Kotian, Anamika Singh, Jyoti Chauhan, Sejal Dsilva, Manthan Patel, Joseph Aloocaran, Pratik Tandel, and Divya Vijayan.

About the reviewers

Raj Chaudhuri has been exploring the IT industry, in various roles, for three decades now. He specializes in simplifying technology and mapping it to real human or organizational needs. Although he focuses mainly on open source technology these days, he still maintains a connection to his first love, Microsoft. He is keenly interested in increasing efficiency in all aspects of IT.

Chantal Bossé has been sharing her passion for visual communications and technology through her business, CHABOS, since 2004. As a presentation and visual communication leader, TEDx speaker coach, Microsoft Office Apps & Services MVP, and expert trainer on the LinkedIn Learning platform, she helps speakers and small businesses improve their PowerPoint presentation, public speaking, and Microsoft 365 and Teams skills. Her goal is to help clients increase their bottom line by leveraging the power of their Microsoft 365 applications. CHABOS' mission is to help small businesses and end users be more empowered and efficient with communication and collaborative technologies.

Vesa Nopanen is an experienced modern work principal consultant at Sulava Oy. Combining an understanding of business needs with technology expertise and vision enables him to help customers to succeed and grow. Vesa is very passionate about Microsoft Teams because it enables us to work together in a modern and hybrid-working world. He also has expertise and experience with Power Platform, Microsoft Viva, change management, and Office 365.

Vesa is also a blogger, an active member of the Microsoft Teams Community, an organizer at Teams Nation, and the founder of Teams Finland. He is also often a speaker at various community and Microsoft events, such as Microsoft Ignite.

Table of Contents

2

Components of Work

3

Creating Content for Effective Communication

4

Intelligent Data Analysis

5

Managing Files Efficiently

Section 2: Efficient Collaboration

6

Time and Task Management

7

Efficient Teamwork and Meetings

Section 3: Integration

8
Automating Work without Programming

9
Putting It All Together

10

Maximizing Efficiency across the Organization

Other Books You May Enjoy

Index

Preface

Everyone wants to grow. We are continuously striving to optimize processes, reduce errors, improve quality, and increase efficiency – in every aspect of business (and life) – except for one technology, Microsoft Office.

Over 1 billion people use it for a few hours every day. So why don't they try to improve their efficiency in using Office apps? Well, the work is getting done and the output is correct. Everyone seems to assume that because their method is working, it must be the best and only way. Maybe that was true on day one when you discovered it by trial and error.

But Microsoft has been adding thousands of features and apps to the Office platform over decades. Not every user has kept pace with it. Having worked with over 400,000 professionals over 30 years, I can confidently say that most processes are inefficient.

I feel sad that so many people are wasting precious time and effort every day because they do not know that there is a better, smarter, or faster way available to get the work done. The result? Without realizing it, they are wasting the most precious resource – time. This has a lot of side effects – overwork, stress, work-life imbalance, and burnout.

You cannot purchase time. But you can create time by working more efficiently. If you have extra time, I am sure you will use it constructively to drive your growth.

My objective is to gift every Office user with at least 20 minutes of extra time every day. You cannot reach 1 billion people by conducting live sessions or videos. That is why I wrote this book.

The Office platform is now known as Microsoft 365, and it consists of 25 apps. I selected the most powerful features across all these apps that *every* user should be aware of.

Conducting a live session is easy. That is what I have been doing for 3 decades. Writing a book is tough. I realized it the hard way while writing this book. I have spent 1 year refining the content.

This is not a user manual. The book teaches you how to learn while you work. It will help you work smarter and grow faster.

Who this book is for

If you use Microsoft Office on a regular basis, this book is for you. MS Office is no longer just Word, Excel, PowerPoint, and Outlook. It is a collection of 25 useful apps. It is now known as Microsoft 365.

You will learn about the benefits each app has to offer. This will help you use the right tool in the right situation. That is efficiency.

Just read the book. Each topic starts with a need and then shows the efficient solution. While reading the book, do not worry about performing each activity hands-on. As long as you know the feature is there, you can always use it when needed. Focus on reading the entire book from a need-solution point of view. That will give you more ideas about where you can use the relevant features in your own context.

What this book covers

Chapter 1, Fortunately, You're Inefficient!, covers the concept of inefficiency and helps you identify areas of improvement.

Chapter 2, Components of Work, introduces all the apps available under Microsoft 365. It also covers some efficiency boosters that are applicable across multiple apps.

Chapter 3, Creating Content for Effective Communication, shows how to create documents, web pages, emails, flow charts, and presentations efficiently.

Chapter 4, Intelligent Data Analysis, is about data. It covers how to import and clean up data and how to analyze data in Excel and Power BI.

Chapter 5, Managing Files Efficiently, explains why it is important that we keep our files on OneDrive for Business. We explore the benefits as well as security advantages of cloud storage.

Chapter 6, Time and Task Management, highlights how to manage your task list and block time to execute work efficiently. We also cover work delegation and monitoring.

Chapter 7, Efficient Teamwork and Meetings, explains how to enhance teamwork and project management using the Teams platform. The efficient meeting life cycle is also included.

Chapter 8, Automating Work without Programming, covers how to automate workflows using Power Automate and how to create mobile apps using Power Apps.

Chapter 9, Putting It All Together, explains how to use these apps in an integrated manner. Also included is the Needs-to-Solutions library. This is a list of common needs and the most efficient solutions.

Chapter 10, Maximizing Efficiency across the Organization, shows how to expand the efficiency transformation to your entire department or organization.

To get the most out of this book

This book covers Microsoft 365 apps. Therefore, you will need access to a subscription for Microsoft 365 – ideally, E3 or Business Premium. If you do not have access to a subscription, you can sign up for a free trial from the Microsoft website in your country.

The Office apps should be installed from the Microsoft 365 (or Office 365) web portal. If you have some other version of Microsoft Office on your PC (such as Office 2016, 2019, and so on), some of the features covered in the book may not work.

Download sample files and resources

You can download the supporting files for this book directly from: `https://static.packt-cdn.com/downloads/978-1-80107-226-7_ExerciseFiles.zip`. If there is an update to the files, it will be updated in the downloadable folder.

Download the color images

We also provide a PDF file that has color images of the screenshots and diagrams used in this book. You can download it here: `https://static.packt-cdn.com/downloads/9781801072267_ColorImages.pdf`.

Conventions used

There are a number of text conventions used throughout this book.

`Code in text`: Indicates code words in text, database table names, folder names, filenames, file extensions, pathnames, dummy URLs, user input, and Twitter handles. Here is an example: "Use the `Ch1 - Table not fitting in page.docx` file from the `Chapter 01` folder in the sample files."

Bold: Indicates a new term, an important word, or words that you see onscreen. For instance, words in menus or dialog boxes appear in **bold**. Here is an example: "Open the **Layout** tab and choose **AutoFit | AutoFit Window**."

> **Tips or Important Notes**
> Appear like this.

Get in touch

Feedback from our readers is always welcome.

General feedback: If you have questions about any aspect of this book, email us at customercare@packtpub.com and mention the book title in the subject of your message.

Errata: Although we have taken every care to ensure the accuracy of our content, mistakes do happen. If you have found a mistake in this book, we would be grateful if you would report this to us. Please visit www.packtpub.com/support/errata and fill in the form.

Piracy: If you come across any illegal copies of our works in any form on the internet, we would be grateful if you would provide us with the location address or website name. Please contact us at copyright@packt.com with a link to the material.

If you are interested in becoming an author: If there is a topic that you have expertise in and you are interested in either writing or contributing to a book, please visit authors.packtpub.com.

Share Your Thoughts

Once you've read *Efficiency Best Practices for Microsoft 365*, we'd love to hear your thoughts! Scan the QR code below to go straight to the Amazon review page for this book and share your feedback:

https://packt.link/r/1801072264

Your review is important to us and the tech community and will help us make sure we're delivering excellent quality content.

Section 1: Efficient Content Creation

This section will help you get off to a flying start – with immediate improvement in efficiency. We will learn how to detect inefficiency and how to find the most efficient way to do something. We will also learn how to create several types of content, including documents, spreadsheets, presentations, web pages, emails, survey forms, and reports. Finally, we will see how to store the files we create in an efficient and secure way.

In this section, there are the following chapters:

1
Fortunately, You're Inefficient!

You can save at least 20 minutes every day if you read and follow this book. Welcome to the world of efficiency! The title says that you are inefficient, referring to inefficiency in the context of using Microsoft Office tools.

My apologies if you feel I am being too harsh. I'm not doubting your ability, expertise, domain knowledge, or experience. Just try the efficiency tests in this chapter to understand what I mean by "inefficiency."

When you use any software, such as Office 365, that has thousands of features, inefficiency is inevitable. Why so? Because you can get the same results in multiple ways. We find one of the ways – usually by trial and error – and stick to it. We never try to find out whether there is a better, faster, smarter way.

Exact probability: Let's say one activity can be done in four different ways. Only one of these methods is efficient. You find one of the methods. You have a 25% chance of finding the best method. How many activities do we perform with Office? Let's say 120. What is the chance of finding the best way every time? 5.6597994e-71%, which basically means zero! In fact, with just 7 activities, the probability drops to 0.006%.

> **Note**
> It is statistically impossible to be efficient by using trial and error.

Why did I say "fortunately"? Because you have already taken the first step. You are reading this and thinking about it. Noticing the problem is the first step of solving a problem. By the end of this book, you will be super efficient. You will save an enormous amount of time, which is the immediate reward of efficiency. You can then invest that time in activities that drive your growth or add value to your life. That's fortunate, is it not?

Let's begin your efficiency transformation. The main topics we will cover in this chapter are as follows:

- What's in it for you?
- Evaluating your inefficiency
- Inefficiency audit – how to find your own inefficiency
- Why are there so many features?
- Discovering your needs behind features
- Moving from a vicious cycle to a virtuous cycle
- Frequent questions answered

Technical requirements

The example files used in this chapter are available here in the `Chapter 01` folder: `https://static.packt-cdn.com/downloads/978-1-80107-226-7_ ExerciseFiles.zip`.

There is a separate folder for each chapter. You can download the files as needed.

What will you gain by reading this book?

You will save at least 20 minutes every day by learning and applying the skills explained in the book. What will you do with the time saved? Use it to your advantage!

Finish your backlog, analyze data more effectively, learn additional skills, improve your work-life balance, focus on your hobbies, get additional certifications – the opportunities are almost limitless. The only limiting factor is time. You cannot purchase time.

But you can create time by being more efficient and use it to achieve more and grow faster in your chosen field.

> **What Is Efficiency?**
> Efficiency is putting in less effort and getting a better impact or more output.

Improving efficiency is a simple, two-step process:

1. Detect inefficiency.
2. Learn how to find a more efficient method.

Most people with a PC use Microsoft Office. We usually learn how to use it by trial and error or on the job. Once the job is completed, nobody checks whether there is a better, more efficient way. That is why most activities are inefficient.

Evaluating your efficiency

Remember – inefficiency does not mean that the method is inaccurate or wrong. Your output may be correct, but there is a better, faster, smarter way to do the job. If you knew about the better way, you could have saved time and used it somewhere else to your advantage.

The question is, who is going to tell you that? Is anybody checking how you work using Office tools? Most probably not. You must do it yourself.

Sounds complicated? Not at all. Let's do some quick tests.

Before we go ahead, let's learn exactly what inefficiency means and how much difference efficiency makes. We will take three examples: one with Word, one with Excel, and one with PowerPoint. You can choose which one you want to try.

Fitting a table in a Word doc

When we copy and paste a table from Excel or a web page, it often goes beyond the Word page boundary, like this:

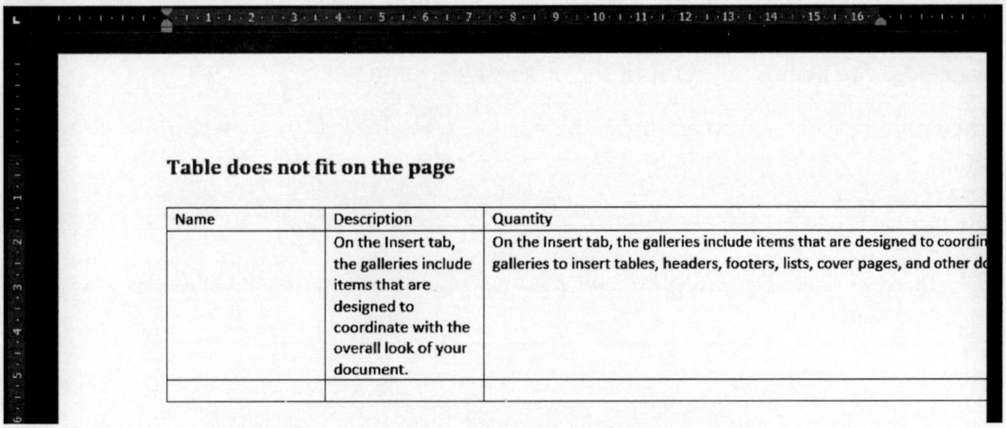

Figure 1.1 – Table exceeding document width

This is a frequent problem. Do you know how to adjust it to fit on the page? Of course, you do. But what process did you use? Think about it.

Use the `Ch1 - Table not fitting in page.docx` file from the `Chapter 01` folder in the sample files.

Here is the efficient method:

1. Click anywhere inside the table. There's no need to select the table, just click inside it.

2. Open the **Layout** tab and choose **AutoFit | AutoFit Window**:

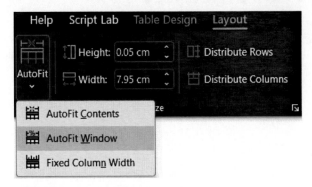

Figure 1.2 – Adjust your table width efficiently

Compare this with your method, and you will know the difference.

Editing formulas in Excel

Every time we add data in Excel, we need to change the formulas that depend upon that range. This is repetitive work. We may not even know how many formulas we need to update. But we have to do this every time data is added. Is that really my job? Am I supposed to help Excel? Or is it the other way around?

Use the sample `Ch 1 - Data and Formulas.xlsx` to get the answer of the above question.

> **Note**
> There is a Trace Dependents option, but most of us do not know about it or use it regularly.

	A	B	C	D	E
1	**Data**				
2				**Formula**	
3	**Product**	**Amt**		75	
4	Mask	10			
5	Gloves	30			**Formula**
6	Sanitizer	20			75
7	Soap	15			
8					
9					
10				**Formula**	
11				75	

Figure 1.3 – Data and formulas

Now try this. After adding the data, create a table and then add formulas. Now add more data; the formulas will update automatically. Watch this video and see for yourself how easy it becomes:

https://hi.switchy.io/fyiww

Why a video? Why not just write the steps here with screenshots? Well, watching a video shows the real, practical way to do it. You learn faster and you can even practice it yourself. Short, fast, and effective.

> **Tip**
> Always use Excel tables. It saves time and promotes accuracy.

Using the Send to Back option in PowerPoint

In this presentation, we have three objects on top of each other. The object in front is easy to edit. But how do we quickly edit the shapes that are behind others? Think about what you would do… manually move them around to remove overlap, or struggle with **Send to Back**?

Use the sample `Ch1 - Send to back.pptx` file from the `Chapter 01` folder.

Of course, there is a better way. Go to the **Home** tab | **Select** | **Selection Pane...**. Now you can see all the items as a list. Select the one you want and edit it. You can edit it even if you cannot see it.

> **Tip**
> Always keep the **Selection Pane** open. PowerPoint editing will become much simpler and faster.

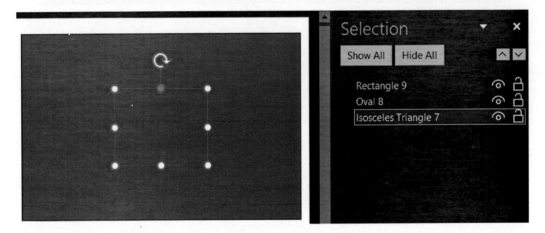

Figure 1.4 – Selection Pane – your best friend in PowerPoint

Now that we are aware of inefficiency, let's see how we can identify it.

Inefficiency audit – how to find your own inefficiency

I can give you many such examples. But that is not the point. How long are you going to depend on me? I want to make you independent and efficient. So, let me show you three powerful ways to find inefficient processes:

- Useless repetition
- Hands versus brain

- Who is helping whom?

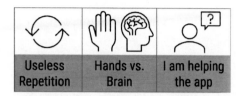

Figure 1.5 – Find inefficiency

Useless repetition

Repetition does not mean inefficiency. In fact, we repeatedly produce the same product or deliver similar service as a part of business, which we get revenue from. That repetition is fine.

Similarly, to manage our business, we must do repetitive things such as pay salaries, check quality, and submit financial reports. This type of repetition is also necessary, not inefficient.

But if you are doing something that is neither getting you revenue nor part of operations, such as manually updating each formula after adding data in Excel, that is inefficient.

Hands versus brain

Here is an example to illustrate this issue. We have 50 numbers. We want to add a formula in the next column and copy it – quite a common requirement. Most people copy a formula by dragging.

Look at the data… for 5,000 rows of data, how long will you have to drag?

While dragging, your hand is busy – but your brain is idle! It is not only a waste of time – it will soon give you arthritis!

The bottom line is, when you notice that you are just using your hands to do some mundane work and your brain is idle, the process is inefficient.

Who is helping whom?

Remember, any software or technology is there to help us. It is not the other way around. Sounds obvious, right? But think about it.

When you were dragging the table columns to fit a table onto a page or using **Send to Back** to make a shape visible, who was helping whom? Were you trying to help Word or PowerPoint?

Is that your job? Absolutely not. So, learn to detect this inefficient behavior. Anytime you feel that you are helping (or even fighting with or struggling with) the software, that means your process is inefficient. It also means that there must be a better way. You just have to find it.

	A	B
2	Amount	Tax
3	352	17.6
4	43	
5	44	
6	41	
5011	42	
5012	52	
5013	55	
5014	19	
5015	67	

Figure 1.6 – Hands versus brain

Is there a better, faster way? Double-click at the bottom-right corner of the sheet

Note: Please insert a space after the phrase 'of the sheet'– it works. Time saved. However, double-clicking is risky because it stops at the first gap it finds.

The most efficient way is to select the full range once and convert it to a table by going to the **Insert** tab and clicking on **Table**. Now, when you add a formula, Excel will copy it automatically. The result? Time saved and greater accuracy. Watch the following video to understand this concept and the solution quickly:

hi.switchy.io/fyihb

We will now see the different features of Office we have available to find our best or most efficient way.

Why are there 14,000+ features?

Yes, there are thousands of features in Office. In 2019, there were more than 14,000 features across all the products.

What are you thinking?

- Oh, that is too much!
- I don't want all these features.
- What I need I already know. That is enough for me.
- Give me only the features I need. It is too confusing.
- This is a feature explosion!

14000+ features
are available

How many do
YOU use?

Figure 1.7 – Underutilization

Now, think about another number – **how many features do you use?**

Over the last 30 years, the answers I have received range from *10* to *130*. The point is that your work is getting done. That is why we get the feeling that "What I know is enough."

Well, I cannot deny that. But let's think a little further. It leads to a subconscious thought – "What I don't know, I don't need."

Does that sound logical? Not at all. How can you say you don't need something that you don't know about?

That is what I call the "inefficient mindset." What if a feature could be useful for you but you refused to notice it?

> **Pro Tip**
> *Figure 1.7* has 14,000 points plotted. I used the SandDance visual in Power BI. It allows you to plot thousands of points in a 3D space and even rotate them interactively. Try it out.

Why do we use only a few features?

When confronted with two numbers – available: 14,000 and used: 150 – what is the typical reaction? Most people try to defend the status quo. They tell me why 150 is enough for them. They may also say "my 150 may be different from your 150," and so on.

But the real question to ask is why did Microsoft create so many features? Do they not know about this reality? Of course, Microsoft is aware.

Adding each feature is a complex and costly process. So why is Microsoft adding so many features? For whom? It is for us – all the users globally – like you and me.

How to learn (to find the best way)

How do you find the most efficient solution for what you need? Without anyone to guide you, how do you find the best way? Usually, we find solutions using one of these methods:

- Ask someone.
- Google it.
- Search the Help file.

Unfortunately, these methods are not effective. Why?

Asking someone is useless because, most probably, that person is also inefficient! You may get a more efficient method from them. But who will tell you if there is an even better way? Why waste time?

Google results depend upon what you search for. If you do not search for `the most efficient way` or `the best` or `the most optimal way`, you are not going to get the best answer on top, and nobody clicks on the next page. That means you are getting "some" answers but not necessarily the most efficient method.

In this case, the Help file is not very useful either. Why? Because for Help to actually help you, you need to type the name of some feature. If you do not know what the feature is, what will you type?

Observing the menus logically

A much simpler way is to assume that if I have a need, Microsoft must have already noticed it and given me a solution. It cannot be in a secret place, right?

What is a solution? A button, a menu option, or a dropdown. So which menu should we look at? The immediate answer to this question is, *observe logically*, and then implement the following:

- Observe and notice all menus logically.
- For local problems, right-click (or click on an ellipsis …).
- For global (bigger) problems, use the menu at the top, called the ribbon.

Local problem – right-clicking

Some options are on the ribbon, but some are not. The concept is simple. If it a local or smaller context, the options are in the right-click menu. If the context is bigger, then the options are in the menu at the top – the ribbon. Things related to the behavior of the application are in **File | Options**.

Once you understand this, you can find the right features quite quickly.

Here is an example. Do you want to change the color of a chart's title? This is a local problem, so right-click on the title – look at all the menus and toolbars that appear and choose the option for you.

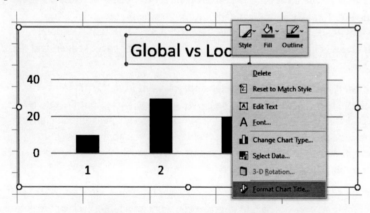

Figure 1.8 – Menu for a local problem

The right-click menu tells you what can you do at that place. That is why it is known as a context menu.

Global problems – top menu

On the other hand, if I want to change the overall design of the chart, that is a larger or global problem. So, I must look for the option in the top menu – the ribbon – in the **Chart Design** tab.

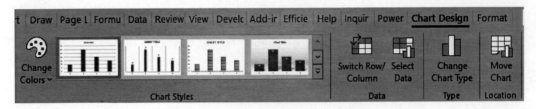

Figure 1.9 – Menu for a global problem

Here is another example. I want to change the red text to blue in this document. There are many places where the red text is present.

Video provides a powerful way to help you prove your point. When you click Online Video, you can paste in the embed code for the video you want to add. You can also type a keyword to search online for the video that best fits your document. To make your document look professionally produced, Word provides header, footer, cover page, and text box designs that complement each other. For example, you can add a matching cover page, header, and sidebar.

Click Insert and then choose the elements you want from the different galleries. Themes and styles also help keep your document coordinated. When you click Design and choose a new Theme, the pictures, charts, and SmartArt graphics change to match your new theme. When you apply styles, your headings change to match the new theme. Save time in Word with new buttons that show up where you need them.

To change the way a picture fits in your document, click it and a button for layout options appears next to it. When you work on a table, click where you

Figure 1.10 – Change red text to blue

The first thought is to select each red area one by one and then change the color.

Repetition + Hands (not brain) + I Am Helping Word = Inefficient Method

The problem is with selecting the red words. Word must have a solution to this problem. Now classify the problem: global or local?

This is a global problem because I want to select text throughout the whole document.

So, I need to use a menu on the top, but which menu?

All editing commands are on the **Home** tab. So, let's go there.

Look at the different buttons and read their names. Do you see any options related to selecting stuff?

That button has a dropdown – let's open that. And amazingly, we have exactly what we need – **Select All Text With Similar Formatting**:

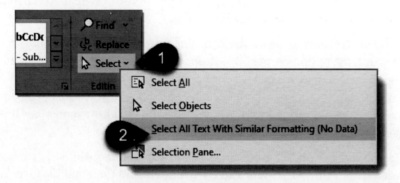

Figure 1.11 – Find the solution

So I click on any red word, choose this option, and then change the color.

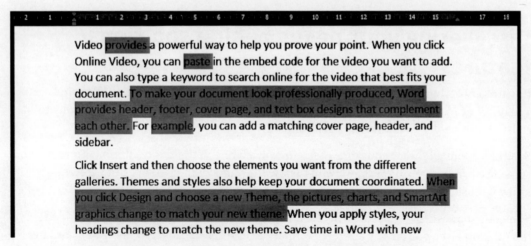

Figure 1.12 – Efficient way of selecting similarly formatted text

> **How to Find the Right Solution**
> If it's a global problem, go to the top menu. If it's a local problem, right-click.

Next, we will see how to change our approach and become super efficient. Once you understand the concept, you can learn on your own for the rest of your life!

Other ways to learn while you work

Here are some more simple and effective ways of learning. They will become clearer as you cover more topics in the book:

- **Observe the mouse cursor and learn**: When the mouse cursor shape changes, the behavior and the right-click menu also change. Check it out and learn.

- **Always open all the drop-down menus**: When there are many options but not enough space, the options appear in a dropdown. Open each dropdown and read the options. In fact, play a game with yourself. Try to predict the options in the dropdown before you open it. If you get all of them right, you win. If you do not guess some of the options, you still win, because you will now remember it very well (a hurt ego is a great teacher!).

- **When you open any dialog, open all tabs and see all the options**: There is no need to try each item. Just notice them and try to understand their significance. You do not have to try each option in the dialog. Just think – when will it be useful?

Now let's learn the process of efficiency transformation.

Discovering your needs behind solutions/ features

If you are not from the IT field, let me explain the concepts of *use case* and *solution*. Whatever needs business users have are called use cases. The IT team develops a way to satisfy those needs. That is called a solution.

So, think about all these thousands of features. Each one of them is a solution. To what? To some need. Whose need? Well, we won't know the name of the person. But we certainly know it must be some user like you and me.

Someone somewhere requested Microsoft to solve their problem and Microsoft added the solution – the button or option – to Office. Over three decades, so many buttons have accumulated and been thrust upon us, leading to confusion.

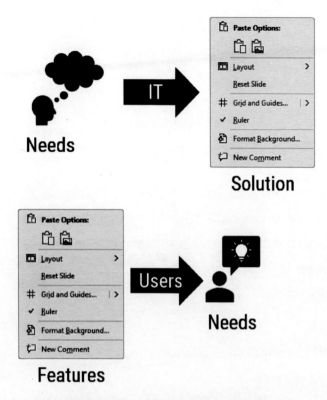

Figure 1.13 – Find needs behind features

So, what can we do at our end? We know that each button is a solution. Now try and find the underlying need. Once you find the need, you can check whether you also have that need. If yes, congratulations – you just found the solution to your need!

If you find that the need is not applicable to your work, no problem. Do not use the feature till the need arises.

> **The Efficient Mindset**
> Find the needs behind every feature.

Now that we are aware of all the different features we have at our disposal, let's see how we can use them to find our best or most efficient solution.

Moving from a vicious to a virtuous cycle

You know how to explore the available features. Here is a recap of how to improve your efficiency using our simple but powerful method.

Vicious cycle:

- We use Office every day to do various activities.
- We have limited time, and we want to use that time to grow in our career and business.
- Each activity we perform using Office is inefficient, which means we are wasting time.
- Because we are wasting time repeatedly, we have less time available.
- This means there is no time to learn the right way or more efficient method.
- Because we are not learning we are not efficient.
- This is the vicious cycle.

Virtuous cycle:

- You find an efficient way to do something.
- That saves you some time.
- You invest some of that time into finding a more efficient method.
- That saves you even more time.
- This is a virtuous cycle.

And that is exactly what we will do in this book. Just keep an open mind, follow the book, and you will see the results for yourself.

> **Stop Ignoring and Start Exploring**
> Ignoring leads to ignorance. Exploration leads to excellence.

Before we proceed, let me address the most common questions I receive. You need not read it in detail. Just browse through the topics. Check the details only if they are relevant to you.

Frequent questions answered

I get these questions very frequently across countries, industries, and roles. Let's handle them upfront. Just browse through the questions and clarify your thoughts.

Which apps/tools are we covering?

Whenever I refer to Microsoft 365, I am referring to all the apps available on the platform at the time of writing this book.

Do not let the number of tools scare you. At this stage, do not say, "I do not need all this."

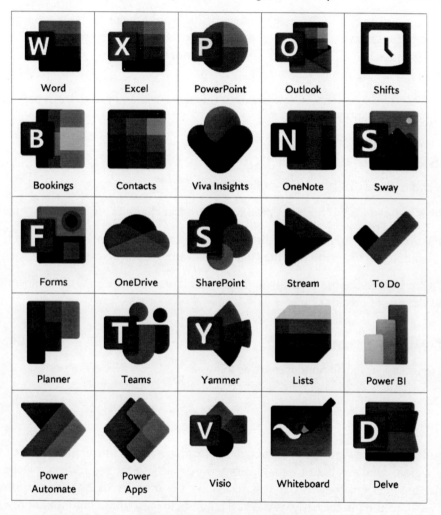

Figure 1.14 – Microsoft 365 apps

As you go through the book, you will understand which app to use when and why. You will learn the most key features for each of these apps. You can then decide which ones are relevant to your work.

How can you cover so many tools in one book?

There are two reasons.

Firstly, we need to at least know what each app does, what need it is serving, and when to use it.

Secondly, we are not covering each app in detail. That would make the book too long and boring. The purpose of this book is to cover the "must-know" features from each of these tools. The objective is not to make you a pro in one tool but make you an expert in using the right tool in the right way.

More importantly, you will learn how *to learn*. This will empower you to learn on your own for the rest of your life!

Is this a tips and tricks book?

No. Tips and tricks are isolated, quick solutions.

This book is not a quick fix. It is a process. It is a mindset change. It is empowerment.

The aim of this book is to make you more efficient and more effective. The topics in this book are handpicked to ensure that they will be relevant to common work needs.

You will learn how to use the tools in an integrated manner to minimize manual work and eliminate wastage of precious time.

What will we not cover?

The two Office apps we will not cover are as follows:

- Access
- Publisher

Why not? Because in a typical business context, they have lost practical utility. Agreed, Access is a great database, but nowadays very few people have the requisite knowledge of proper database design. They tend to use Access like Excel, which defeats the purpose of using it. Furthermore, in the early days, Excel could manage a limited number of rows, so Access was the natural external database. Now, with Power Pivot and data models, the Excel row limit and scalability constraints no longer apply. Therefore, the most common need for using Access no longer exists.

Publisher is designed for creating print and web graphics. It is a great tool. But nowadays, more popular tools exist – Canva, Spark, even PowerPoint. Therefore, I decided not to cover Publisher.

Why are there so many apps? Do I need all of them?

All these apps have a purpose. Microsoft is a professional, smart, and profitable company. You can rest assured that they will not put effort to make apps that have no purpose or benefit.

How to use this book

This book will help you find solutions to your needs.

Each topic in every chapter starts with a need and then shows the solution. If it is your need (requirement/use case), continue reading the topic. If not, go to the next topic.

Also, think about whether someone else around you (colleague, boss, subordinate) has that need. If yes, refer them to the solution.

Do not limit your thinking to the original need or scenario. Think more and find other situations where the same solution/feature may be applicable.

Prerequisites

You need to have a Microsoft 365 subscription and the cloud version of Office installed on the desktop, preferably on Windows 10 or 11. Some features covered in this book may not work on the Mac version of Office.

Traditionally, Office meant Word, Excel, PowerPoint, and Outlook. Microsoft has added more cloud applications to the suite, such as OneDrive, Teams, SharePoint, and Forms. Office and these cloud applications was referred to as Office 365. If you added Windows 10 and Security to the mix, it became Microsoft 365.

Office 365 was recently re-branded as Microsoft 365. Throughout this book, we will refer to it as Microsoft 365.

You must have Office 365 E3 and Microsoft 365 E3 to follow this book. You need to install the desktop version of Office from the Office.com portal.

If you do not have such a license, you can sign up for a trial for Office 365 E3. Use this link to start the trial: `https://www.microsoft.com/en-us/microsoft-365/enterprise/compare-office-365-plans`. To open the site to your country, scroll to the bottom of this page and choose a different location from the dropdown in the bottom-left corner. The free trial gives you a 1-month period to learn.

Log in to the Office.com site using your ID. In the top-right corner, click the **Install Office** button to install the right version of Office on the desktop.

Check the version by going to **File | Accounts**. The version should be **Microsoft 365 Apps for enterprise**.

Figure 1.15 – Office version in File | Accounts

If you have a different version, some of the features covered in this book will not be available.

Summary

In this chapter, we learned why we are inefficient. We learned three powerful ways of detecting inefficiency – useless repetition, who is helping whom, and hands versus brain. Finally, we saw how to find the right solution quickly – either through the top menu or by right-clicking.

Try this every day while you are working. The more you try, the easier it will be to detect problems and find solutions.

Congratulations. You are already on your way to becoming super efficient.

Now we know why Office has so many features – simply because we have so many needs. We may not have noticed many of our own needs, but Microsoft has. Let's take advantage of this and become efficient.

In the next chapter, we will see how to learn features and discover the benefits of using them. This will help you understand the plethora of features in a logical and empowering way.

2
Components of Work

This book is for everyone who uses Office. There is so much variety in what we do – different subject areas, industries, roles, and levels of experience. So how can one book cover all these variations?

The answer is simple. Your work consists of two types: structured and unstructured. The structured part of your work requires knowledge of your subject and industry and the unstructured part of your work is common across the board. We can divide unstructured work into universal activities and needs such as creating files, storing data, teamwork, execution of tasks, and data analysis.

Microsoft built solutions (apps) for these needs and packaged them together into Microsoft 365. Here is a map of the needs and solutions.

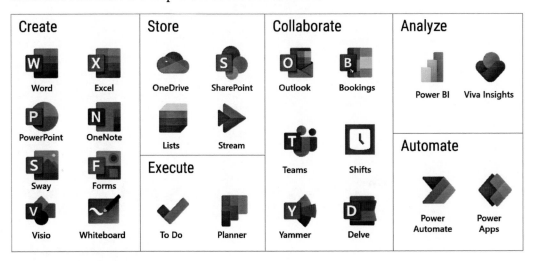

Figure 2.1 – Apps in Microsoft 365 – which tool app to use and when

We will cover the key features of each app in this book. You need not be an expert in these features, but you need to be aware of them. Only then will you be able to use the right tool in the right place and become super-efficient.

The main two topics we'll cover in this chapter are:

- The topics covered in this book
- A primer on efficiency

How is this book organized?

Each chapter covers one common need and the related apps. Everything you see is need-based – identify the need first and then the solution. *Chapter 3, Creating Content for Effective Communication*, to *Chapter 8, Automating Work without Programming*, you can read in any order. Focus on what is more relevant to you. But it is equally important that you at least glance through all chapters and the main topics. This will help you to discover and address your needs related to these powerful features.

Creating files and content

Creating Word, Excel, and PowerPoint files is a common activity. In addition to these, we will also look at some lesser-known but powerful apps such as Sway, Whiteboard, and now, Visio (used for creating flowcharts and process diagrams).

Creating files is easy. With most apps, you select the **File - New** option and start typing. However, to create files efficiently, we need to understand a particularly important concept.

> **The concept**
> You supply the content and then let the app help you to refine it.

You can type, copy-paste, insert pictures, add data – that is your job.

Formatting, layout, calculations, beautification … you *do not* have to put in any manual work. You ask for what you want and the app does it for you. In *Chapter 3, Creating Content for Effective Communication*, we will apply this concept to all the content creation apps.

Now let's see how to store these files efficiently and safely.

Data management and analysis

Data is everywhere and it is always increasing. However, just having data is not enough. We need to understand it and take correct decisions and actions based on it. We spend a lot of time getting data and analyzing it. How can we make this process efficient? That is what we will cover in *Chapter 4, Intelligent Data Analysis*. We will focus on the following:

- How to capture data efficiently:

  - Good and bad data formats

  - The right tool for data capture (forms versus tabular)

- How to clean data efficiently (without manual work or macros)

- How to analyze data and find all useful things from it (reports or dashboards)

- Flexible analysis and interactive dashboards using Pivot Tables and Power BI

You will save an enormous amount of time and increase the impact of your analyses after reading this chapter.

Storing and managing files

Storing files on a local drive is popular but it has many disadvantages. Storing them on the cloud is safer and more efficient. We do use cloud storage. But not efficiently (sigh!). In this chapter, we will cover all the benefits of storing files on the cloud (OneDrive, Teams, or SharePoint).

> **Important Note**
> Storing files on the cloud has twelve benefits. Storing files on a local drive has
> no benefits!

The cloud never sleeps. It is always *on*. Anybody with access to files can view or edit the files at any time. That is why we do not need to *send* files anymore. Sending their address (link) is enough. Attachments are inefficient and insecure. Sending links is efficient and secure. But it takes a lot of convincing for people to do this confidently. Do not worry. After reading *Chapter 5, Managing Files Efficiently*, you will understand what you have been missing all along.

> **Always Send Links – No More Attachments**
> In specific cases, we need to send files as attachments for legal, statutory, or
> operational requirements. That is fine, but as a rule, share links.

Why do we create and store files? It is a part of our job, work, business activities, and so on. So the next step is to understand how to manage our work effectively.

Managing time and tasks

There are two types of work: my work and teamwork.

My work means the work I execute. Teamwork means a group of people is responsible for getting the work done together.

There are four components of managing your work:

- Creating and keeping a master list of pending work (Outlook Tasks):

    - Converting emails to Tasks (Outlook inbox)

    - Converting meeting action points to Tasks (OneNote)

- Finding time to do the work (Outlook Calendar)

- Delegating work without sending emails (Outlook Tasks)

- Monitoring task execution:

    - On desktop (Outlook)

    - On mobile (To Do app)

And of course, to do all this work, you need time. In *Chapter 6, Time and Task Management*, you will learn how you can manage your work and your time effectively.

Managing teamwork and meetings

In *Chapter 7, Efficient Teamwork and Meetings*, we will focus on managing teamwork effectively – whether you are in the office, at home, or traveling. Even if you are a one-person company, you will still need to work with vendors, customers, suppliers, consultants, and so on. There are two types of Teamwork:

- Simple teamwork:

  - This is coordination, discussion, providing information/help to each other – just the routine part of working with others.

  - Depending upon the urgency of what you need, choose the right tool or app.

  - This type of work can involve chat, meetings, discussions, data capture, and file sharing.

- Multiple related tasks:

  - It involves a shared task list – typically called a project plan.

  - Everyone needs to be coordinated and know the current status of the tasks.

We will cover related topics such as Contacts, Shifts, Bookings, and Yammer.

Automating repetitive tasks

Do not worry, you do not need to be a programmer or an IT person to learn this. It is possible to simplify or even end repetitive work quite easily using Power Automate app:

- Repetitive tasks that cannot be automated:

  - **Copy-paste**: Copy-paste is the most common activity here. We will cover many powerful and efficient ways of copy-pasting data. We will also cover how to get multiple clipboards instead of just one.

  - **Undo**: **Undo** is also a common action. Do we use **Undo** only to recover from a mistake? Not at all. We will learn this powerful lesson as well.

  - **Shortcuts**: Everyone wants to know keyboard shortcuts. But which shortcuts do you need? That nobody else can tell you. Right? Therefore, I will help you learn exactly the shortcuts *you* need. We will also learn how to have keyboard shortcuts even for buttons that do not have their own shortcut.

- Finding tasks for which automation is possible:

  Often, we repeat the same processes periodically. For example, cleaning input data that comes in every month or sending thank you emails to customers who responded to a survey. It is worth checking whether we can automate such work.

We will explore a new way of automating things across apps – using Power Automate. No programming knowledge is needed. We will cover this powerful tool in *Chapter 8, Automating Work without Programming*.

Putting it all together

Once we learn about individual apps, it is time to use them in the right way. In *Chapter 9, Putting It All Together*, we will learn which tool to use when. We will also see how these tools work with each other – integration. I have also included an efficiency ready reckoner with common needs and efficient solutions.

Maximizing efficiency across the organization

Finally, in *Chapter 10, Maximizing Efficiency across the Organization*, I will share best practices, proven techniques, and practical approaches for making everyone in the organization more efficient.

Often, despite buying technology and tools, the utilization is still poor. This is a waste of money, time, and human effort. You will learn about many quick-win ideas, gamification, and more in this chapter.

> **Features may not match**
>
> We are going to cover 25 apps in this book. All these apps are evolving rapidly. Microsoft gets lots of requests for new features and enhancements all the time. Therefore, the features that I am writing about in this book may change over time. The screenshots may also look different due to changes in the user interface.
>
> It is also possible that your IT policy restricts some features or apps. Many restrictions may apply due to security or compliance reasons, based upon your organizational context.
>
> The important thing is to learn to learn. That way, you will be able to navigate an ever-changing landscape of products, apps, and features.

Keep reading to learn some tips and tricks that will give a boost to your efficiency.

Efficiency primer

Before we learn about all the apps, here are some common things you should know or do to improve your productivity. This knowledge will help you with Windows, Office, and other apps.

You are the boss

This is an important and fundamental concept to understand:

1. You supply things that the app cannot.
2. You *don't* do things that the app can do better than you!
3. You demand what you want, and the app will do it for you.

> *You* **are the boss**
>
> You should not help the app. You demand and the app will deliver. It is a simple division of labor. You supply the content; the app does the rest!

Sounds philosophical, ambiguous, or confusing? Do not worry. Just read on...

Mouse cursor shape

The mouse cursor keeps changing its shape depending upon where it is. Start noticing it.

Why? Because when the shape changes, its job changes. It behaves differently. Notice this consciously. If the shape changes and you do not know what it does, find out. That is how even the mouse cursor can be your teacher!

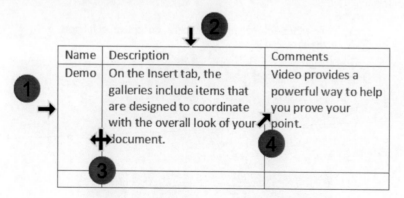

Figure 2.2 – Mouse cursor shape changing

For example, in this table, the first cursor selects the entire row, the second one selects the entire column, the third one helps you resize the column, and the fourth one selects the content of that specific cell (especially useful for cells containing lots of content).

There is more. Whenever the mouse cursor's shape changes, the right-click menu also changes. Try it out. That is why the right-click menu is known as the context menu – it understands the context and shows what you can do in the current context.

If you are showing the use of some application during a meeting (online or in person using projection), increase the mouse cursor size and change its color. This makes it easy for the audience to follow your actions. Go to **Windows Settings | Mouse Pointer | Increase Size to 2 or 3 and change Color**. This is also useful if you want to record the screen activity and create instructional videos.

Using dialogs efficiently

When a separate window opens with the **OK / Cancel** buttons, it is a dialog. There are two simple shortcuts here. You *do not* have to click the **OK** button. Notice that it has a thick border. The shortcut to choose **OK** is to press the *Enter* key.

Pressing *ESC* chooses **Cancel**.

> **Note**
> While we are at it, notice the underline below **Open** and **Browse....** The shortcut is to use the *Alt* key with the corresponding letter.

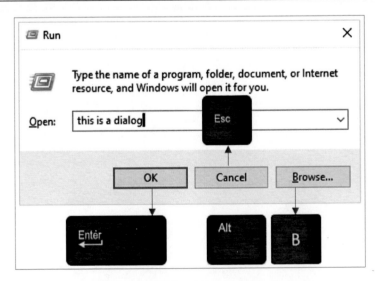

Figure 2.3 – OK and Cancel shortcuts

Another point to remember is to open dropdowns using *Alt* + the *down arrow*. There's no need to move your hand away from the keyboard and click using the mouse.

Using the taskbar

The taskbar is where you see the **Start** button (1) and all other running app icons (2). On the right side, you see a lot of useful information, such as the time, volume, network, and so on. This area is the System Tray or Taskbar Notification Area.

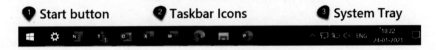

Figure 2.4 – Windows taskbar

Let's use this area efficiently:

- Remove unwanted icons from here. Go to **Settings** in Windows and search for Notification area. Remove the icons you don't want to see. The idea is to reduce visual clutter and increase focus.

- Make icons smaller (right-click and figure out). In this way, you can view more icons in the same area.

Pinning apps to your taskbar

The apps that you use often should *not* be launched from the **Start** menu. When using it for the first time, do the following:

1. Go to the **Start** menu and find the app but *do not* click on it.
2. Right-click on it and choose **Pin to Taskbar**.
3. The icon now appears on the taskbar.
4. Click it to start the app – a single click. Efficient!

When the app has files open, there is a small bar below the icon.

Rearranging taskbar icons on demand

The order of taskbar icons can be changed – just drag and drop them. Change the order to suit your work. Drag the apps you are actively using to the rightmost side. Do this for every important, time-consuming activity.

For example, when I am writing a blog, I need the browser, PowerPoint, and OneNote.

Figure 2.5 – Pinned apps on the taskbar

When I am creating content for YouTube, I need a browser, PowerPoint, Camtasia, and SnagIT.

Figure 2.6 – Rearrange apps on the taskbar

This way, your navigation between applications becomes simple and more logical.

If you use multiple monitors, you should show the icon only on the monitor where the app is displayed by going to **Windows Settings | Taskbar settings | Show Taskbar buttons on – Taskbar where the window is open**. If you are sharing one of the screens, then you want to show all icons only on the non-presenting screen.

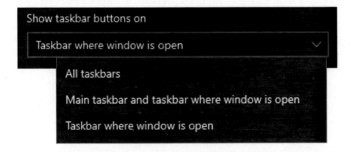

Figure 2.7 – Taskbar icon display settings

Using System Tray icons

The icons on the right side of the taskbar are called tray icons. The volume, date, and network are shown by default. You can see more icons when you click the up arrow (1). Find the OneDrive icon (2). We will need to use it in upcoming chapters.

Figure 2.8 – OneDrive icon

When to use a single click versus a double-click

To open hyperlinks, we use a single click. Menu (Ribbon) buttons require a single click. Starting/opening a program from the desktop requires a double-click.

Do not get confused – try a single click, and if it does not work, double-click.

> **Note**
> Is there a triple-click? Yes! In Word, a triple-click selects a paragraph.

Ctrl + Click on any hyperlink to open it in a new tab.

If you have a mouse wheel with a click, map that to *Ctrl + Click* using the mouse software. It is very handy while browsing.

Using the burger, waffle, and overflow menus

Mobile apps have less space to work with. Therefore, the menus are much smaller to save space. Typically, the menu in a mobile app is just three horizontal lines – this is the **burger menu** (1).

We cannot use a mouse with cell phones. Therefore, right-click is not possible. It is just three dots (…), also called an **ellipsis** or the **overflow menu** (2). Like with the right-click, always click on the three dots to learn what options are available. Sometimes these three dots are horizontal and sometimes they are vertical.

Figure 2.9 – Burger and ellipsis menus

If there are many related apps, you get a square made of dots (App Launcher) – this is the waffle menu.

Figure 2.10 – Waffle menus

All apps have settings. Usually, the icon for the settings menu is a gear wheel, a cog wheel, or a sprocket – like this ⚙. In this book, we will refer to it as the settings wheel.

Important keyboard shortcuts

Here are a couple of shortcuts to get us started:

- Paste special: *Shift + Ctrl + V*
- Insert hyperlink: *Ctrl + K*

You might already know that *Ctrl + C* is for copy, *Ctrl + V* is for paste, *Ctrl + X* is for cut, and *Ctrl + Z* is for undo. Why *Z*? Because it is the key nearest to the *Ctrl* key – so it is the easiest key combination to press. It is sad that we need to use undo so often. Undo frequency is a good indicator of inefficiency!

Wherever there are paragraphs, use *Shift + Alt +* the *up* or *down arrow.* See what happens. This works with Word tables as well! (It does not work with PowerPoint tables or Excel.)

How can you learn shortcuts? Just notice the tooltips of commonly used buttons. If there is a keyboard shortcut, it will be visible in the tooltip.

Creating custom toolbars

What if you click a button often, and it does not have a keyboard shortcut? No problem – right-click on it and choose **Add to Quick Access Toolbar (QAT)**.

Add often used commands here to create a custom toolbar for all Office apps. Now, press the *Alt* key and see the magic. All your custom buttons get a number. For example, in the following screenshot, *Alt 3* is **Wrap Text**. This is how you get keyboard shortcuts for commands that do not have keyboard shortcuts.

Figure 2.11 – Press Alt key for QAT shortcuts

If you have a lot of buttons in the QAT, right-click on it and show it below the ribbon. That way, it does not encroach upon the title bar and filename.

Right-click on the QAT and customize it. Rearrange the buttons in such a way that the first nine buttons are the most often used commands. That way, you get *Alt 1* to *Alt 9* as convenient shortcuts.

How and when to use the Shift, Ctrl, and Alt keys

These work differently with other keystrokes and with the mouse:

- The *Shift* key with the mouse is usually the constraint key – draw perfect circles and squares while pressing *Shift*.

- *Ctrl* changes the behavior while dragging. While dragging an item, press the *Ctrl* key to copy the item (instead of moving it).

- While selecting items such as files or Excel cells, *Ctrl* allows the selection of non-contiguous items.

- Use the *Alt* key is used to see all the keyboard shortcuts in Office tools. (Or any application that has a Ribbon type of menu). Press only the *Alt* key and release it. You will see all menus with keyboard shortcuts. That way, you do not have to memorize keyboard shortcuts.

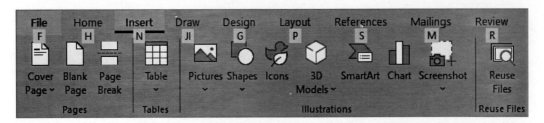

Figure 2.12 – Press the Alt key to see keyboard access keys

Using Alt + Tab and Windows + Tab

While working on multiple apps, use the *Alt + Tab* key to shift from one application to another. Keep pressing *Alt* and press and release *Tab* – keep switching applications. When you reach the desired app, release the *Alt* key.

Do not want to keep the *Alt* key pressed? No problem. Press the *Windows* key and *Tab*. See all the apps in preview (thumbnail) mode and click the one you want to use.

Options available in the Office Ribbon

The Ribbon is the official name for MS Office menus – because it is long and broad. Each item in the menu (Ribbon) is known as a tab. **Home**, **Insert**, **Draw**, and so on are tabs.

Figure 2.13 – Ribbon and tabs

Each tab has lots of related buttons. Vertical lines separate them into groups of related buttons. Each group has a name. When you are searching for some button, look at the group names first. Find the most relevant group and then look at the buttons.

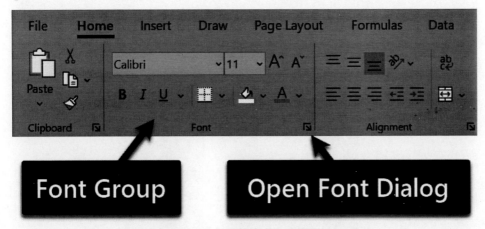

Figure 2.14 – Command group and dialog launcher

If the group has a detailed dialog, then you see a small arrow in the bottom-right corner. In this case, the **Font** group has a dialog associated with it. We can open it using the arrow icon. The technical name for these icons is the **dialog launcher**.

Using the File menu efficiently

With Office apps, the **File** menu has a lot of stuff to show. Therefore, it occupies the whole screen. Three key areas we need to know are the following:

- **File | Info**: Everything about the currently open file shows up here. All properties are visible and editable from here. You can also remove unwanted or potentially sensitive data from here using **Info – Check for Issues | Inspect Document**. This helps you remove multiple items from the document instantly. For example, you can remove all properties, all notes from a presentation, all comments and tracked changes. If you want the original content, make a copy of the file first and then run the **Inspect Document** option on it.

  Check for Issues | Check Accessibility – is very useful. You must run it and check if people with disabilities can consume your content easily. Look at the suggestions and repair the document accordingly. That is how you contribute to making the world an inclusive place.

- **File | New | Templates: File | New** shows lots of useful templates. Explore the categories and remember to use them when needed. Templates saved by you will appear under **Personal** section as shown in the following figure.

Figure 2.15 – Personal templates

> **Note**
> MaxOffice is my organization name. You can deploy organizational templates here. If you are from IT, find out how to deploy templates centrally from here: `https://docs.microsoft.com/en-us/sharepoint/ organization-assets-library`.

- **File | Options**: You often need to go to **Options** to change the overall behavior of the app. There are too many options, but do not get confused. Look at the categories on the left side first. That is all you need to know at this stage.

Pinning often used files and folders

In the **File** menu, each file and folder has a pin icon. For frequent files and folders, pin them.

You can also pin items to taskbar icons. Right-click on the app icon to see recently opened files. Pin them so that you can open the app and the file in one click. Even better!

Figure 2.16 – Pin frequently used documents

Remember to unpin them when you do not need to open the file often. For example, when you finish a project, send the final document, or complete a contract.

Getting familiar with the status bar

All desktop Office apps have a status bar at the bottom. It shows a lot of useful information and has some actionable buttons, typically on the right side.

Figure 2.17 – Word status bar

Right-clicking on the status bar gives you more options. We will explore a few of these options later, in *Chapter 3, Creating Content for Effective Communication*. At this stage, just notice all the components shown in the status bar.

Figure 2.18 – Zoom slider on the status bar

> **Note**
> Most Office apps have the zoom slider on the right side of the status bar.

In Outlook, we often use the **Reading Pane** on the right (or at the bottom). The zoom level in this pane is customizable. Right-click on the status bar and choose **Zoom Slider**. Once you find the best zoom level, double-click on the zoom percentage number, and choose **Remember my preference**.

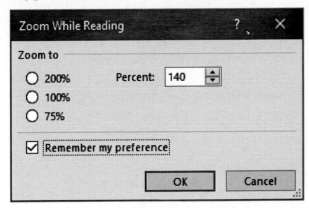

Figure 2.19 – Zoom level for reading pane

Getting twenty-four clipboards

Yes, with Word, Excel, and PowerPoint, you can get 24 clipboards. Just click on the button as shown here:

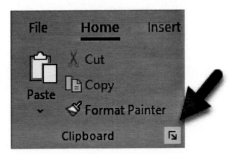

Figure 2.20 – Get more clipboards

Now, onwards, whatever you copy will go to separate clipboards. You can keep copying multiple things and then paste all of them at once.

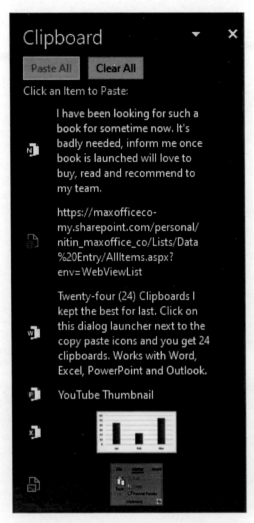

Figure 2.21 – Multiple clipboards

You can copy from anywhere (not just Office apps), but the multiple clipboards are available only within Office apps. Try it out. You will love it.

If you choose the regular **Paste** option or use the *Ctrl + V* shortcut, it will paste the last clipboard – as expected. But you can go to the other copied items and paste them from the Office **Clipboard** window. Depending upon where you are pasting to, you can also **Paste All** of the copied items in one stroke.

While we are at it, pressing the *Windows* key + *V* also gives you multiple clipboards at the Windows level. The first time you press *Windows* + *V*, it will ask you to enable the feature. It is known as clipboard history.

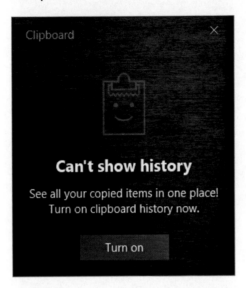

Figure 2.22 – Windows-level clipboards

Using the Microsoft SwiftKey keyboard app on Android and iOS, you can sync the clipboard from a PC to a cell phone and vice versa. See this article for details: `https://support.swiftkey.com/hc/en-us/articles/360050207692-How-to-use-Microsoft-SwiftKey-to-copy-and-paste-across-your-devices.`

Windows grouping

Often, we need to have two windows side by side. This is useful when comparing two documents or copy-pasting from one document to another.

Here is how you do it quickly. Go to the first app and press the *Windows* key with the left arrow to move the current app to the left half of the screen. It will then ask what you want to put on the right half of the screen. Choose the other app. It will snap to the right half of the screen. Now you can see both windows without overlap.

Exercise: Learn what the Windows key with the up arrow or down arrow does

With Windows 11, this process has become even simpler. You can just hover the mouse over the maximize button of any window. It will now show various window grouping options. Choose where you want the window to fit and arrange it instantly.

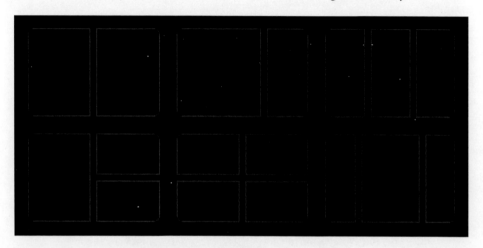

Figure 2.23 – Windows 11 Snap Groups

Snap Groups are visible on the taskbar as well. You can minimize the entire group in one action, instead of minimizing each window separately. Snap Groups are super useful and efficient.

How can you increase concentration?

You can use these three simple techniques:

- Minimize all windows – *Windows key* + *M*.
- Use Windows Focus Assist to disable distractions and notifications.
- Minimize notifications .

Reading efficiently using Immersive Reader

While reading long documents or lengthy emails, we need to concentrate. Immersive Reader is a great tool to help grasp content quickly and without distractions. Word, OneNote, Teams, Outlook, and Edge support Immersive Reader.

It shows the long text (document, web page, email, and so on) in fullscreen mode to help you focus. You can adjust the column width and number of lines shown at a time. If you understand better by hearing rather than reading, Immersive Reader can read the text aloud. You can even adjust the speed of reading and choose a male or female voice.

In Word and OneNote, go to the **View** tab. With email, Immersive Reader is available in the **Message** tab.

With Teams, hover over any message, click the ellipsis (overflow menu), and choose Immersive Reader.

Figure 2.24 – Immersive Reader in Teams

Show it to your kids as well. It has a picture dictionary and translation feature. It is great for learning languages and increasing the comprehension of any subject.

Using the Start menu to search

Open the **Start** menu and type the search text. Choose the kind of search you want to perform – **Photos**, **Documents**, **Music**, **Video**, **Web**, and so on. Sure, you already use this type of search, but there is more.

File Explorer search is more flexible and powerful compared to the **Start** menu search. Press *Ctrl + F* to search within File Explorer. Here are a few examples of how you can get correct and specific search results:

You want to search for	Type this
PowerPoint presentation with the word **Demo** in its name.	`demo pptx`
All images with the word **Birthday** in the filename. *You do not remember whether these are JPG, GIF, or PNG… you do not need to!*	`birthday kind: pictures`
All videos with the word **Graduation** in the filename.	`graduation kind: video`
All files with the words **Project Report** in the filename that are large	`project report size: large`
Presentations created in the year 2018	`Ppt* created:2018`

You can learn the detailed syntax here: `https://docs.microsoft.com/en-us/windows/win32/lwef/-search-2x-wds-aqsreference`.

The Everything app

Everything is an amazing search app. It is so good that even though it is not a part of Microsoft 365, I am adding it here. Download and install the Everything app from this link: `https://www.voidtools.com/`. This app does not search inside file content, but it is extremely fast for filename and attribute (dates, sizes, types of files, and so on) searches.

Once you start this application, it is ready to search in a few seconds. Go to the **Help** menu and see **Search Syntax** to learn more.

Here is a query that returns only PNG images created in 2021:

```
ext:png dm:2021
```

Right-click the search results to learn all the possible actions. One of the most useful actions is **Copy Full Name to Clipboard**. Often, when you are opening files in other apps, you forget the exact folder and filenames. Use the Everything app to find a file instantly. Use the *Shift + Ctrl + C* shortcut to copy the file path and paste it into the filename area of any file: **File | Open dialog.**

Summary

"Why did I not know this earlier?!" Did you have this thought at least a few times?

We have learned twenty-three extremely useful skills. You are already more efficient. But this is just the beginning. Try these skills out while working, teach others, and get ready to explore the Microsoft 365 apps in the upcoming chapters.

Let's learn how to manage individual work components in detail. In the next chapter, we will see how to create content more efficiently using Word, PowerPoint, and other tools.

Even if you use one of the tools more than others, just go through all of the tools. I have hand-picked the most important and useful features for you. Let's dive into it.

3
Creating Content for Effective Communication

In this chapter, we will learn how to create six types of content: documents, emails, notes, presentations, flowcharts, and web pages. We create content to communicate with others. Therefore, we will learn how to do the following:

- Create content efficiently.
- Make it easier for others to understand and use our content.

There are two common concepts for efficient content creation: *using the right tool/feature in the right place* and *reuse*.

You, as the creator, supply the base material – text, images, tables, videos, links, and so on. You *should not* perform any work manually that the app can do better than you. This includes formatting, coloring, and setting the fonts and layout. The app should help you. You should not help the app.

The second concept is about reuse. If you need to use the same content in multiple places (paragraph, table, diagram, email reply, and so on), you should not copy and paste it from the original. There is always a faster, smarter way to reuse existing content.

In this chapter, we will cover the following:

Objective	App
Create documents	Word
Create emails	Outlook
Capture notes and link notes to meetings	OneNote
Create flowcharts and process diagrams	Visio
Create presentations, interactive slides, illustrations, narrated videos, animated GIFs, and self-running kiosks	PowerPoint
Create web pages instantly without programming	Sway

This chapter will help you create better-quality documents faster – with minimal effort. Less effort, more impact.

Even if you do not use all of these tools, please go through the entire chapter. It is possible that when you read about an app you have not used before, it will help you visualize where you can use it.

Sometimes, we are using the wrong app without knowing it! A classic example is that many of us use shapes in PowerPoint to create flowcharts. You may not know that a more comprehensive and easier-to-use app called Visio is now available in Microsoft 365.

Let's start with Word. Most people think that they know all there is about Word already. Get ready for a major surprise!

> **Please Note**
>
> Throughout this book, I am referring to the Microsoft 365 version of Office apps on Windows 10 (or above) – unless otherwise stated. Make sure you go to any Office app – Word, for example – and sign in to your Microsoft 365 account on the desktop: **File | Account | Add Account | Add a service | OneDrive for Business**. Some features may not be available in other (non-English) language editions of Microsoft 365 apps.

Technical requirement

The sample files used in this chapter are available here in the Chapter 03 folder: https://static.packt-cdn.com/downloads/978-1-80107-226-7_ExerciseFiles.zip.

Professional documents with Word

Often, we feel that Word is so simple that there is nothing more to learn there. But that is not the case. Let's learn how Word can make your documents shine. Whether it is your CV, a customer proposal, or a project report, your document can make you stand out from the competition – with blessings from Word!

Objectives

Here are four simple goals for a document:

- The document should look *professional*.
- It should be *easy* to read.
- We should choose the *right words* in the right place.
- All this should happen with minimal manual effort.

Word has solutions for all your needs. You just ask Word to do what you need by selecting the right menu or command. That is all there is to it.

Styles – no more manual formatting

The most time-consuming job is applying formatting manually. To save you that trouble, Word has styles. There are many styles in Word, which give you ready-to-use formatting with just a click.

Noticing where styles are

Go to the **Home** tab and then the **Styles** group. Look at the styles available. Open the dropdown and get familiar with what is available. You don't have to use all of them. But usually, we need at least three of them – **Heading 1** for main topics, **Heading 2** for subtopics, and **Title**, for the title. Of course, for more complex documents, there are up to nine levels of headings.

Figure 3.1 – Word styles

Even if you do not use a style, the **Normal** style is the default. Once you start using styles, there is no need for repeated manual formatting.

Using styles

Each formal document has a title. So, write the title, click anywhere inside it, and select the **Title** style (no need to select the text).

This is a Title

This is Heading1 (main topic)
This is normal style (regular text)

Figure 3.2 – Styles in a document

For main topics, use **Heading 1**, for subtopics use **Heading 2**, and so on.

Are two levels not enough? If you use **Heading 2**, then Word reveals **Heading 3**. A maximum of nine levels is available – which is more than enough for most complex documents.

> **Note**
> Apply heading styles *while* you type the document content.

Here are the benefits of using styles.

Instant table of contents

Create a document with some headings and then go to the **References** tab, click on **Table of Contents**, and choose **Contents**. Miraculously, you get the table of contents instantly and automatically.

> **Warning**
> The table of contents does not update automatically. Before sending or printing the document, right-click on the table of contents and choose **Update Field | Update entire table**. That's it.

Instant navigation – no more Find Next

Say you want to go to a specific topic in a long document. How? Don't even think about using *Ctrl + F* and **Find Next** – that is inefficient. Remember our criteria – repetition, hands vs. brain, and who is helping whom? All of them apply here.

Go to **View | Navigation Pane** and see what happens. An interactive table of contents is shown on the left side of the document.

Tip

You are likely to use **Navigation Pane** regularly. Therefore, it is convenient to add it to the Quick Access Toolbar; see *Chapter 2, Components of Work*, the *Creating custom toolbars* section. Right-click on **Navigation Pane** in the **View** tab and select **Add to Quick Access Toolbar**.

Rearranging a document without copy and pasting

Try this out: drag a heading in **Navigation Pane** and drop it in a different place. The entire content below it is instantly rearranged – without cumbersome selection and copy and paste! By the way, this feature has been there for over 10 years.

At this point, most people think *"Oh dear... what was I doing for 10 years!"*. Never mind. There is no *undo* in life. But your future is already efficient. Enjoy it.

Exercise: Try to Retrofit Styles in Older Documents

Find documents that have manually formatted headings. Make a copy. Click on one of the manually formatted headings, then go to **Home | Select | Select Text with Similar Formatting**. Now apply **Heading 1**. Repeat for other headings. Now you can get all the benefits of styles for older documents as well.

Understanding sections

You cannot change the layout of a single page in Word. But you can do it at the section level. Sections are an often unknown but extremely useful feature.

Check whether you need any of these

If your answer to any of the following is yes, then you need to use sections:

- Do you need one (or a few) pages to be in landscape?
- Do you need the first few pages to be without page numbers and start numbering after, say, the table of contents?
- Do you want multiple columns within regular text?

How can we see sections?

Understand this – a document has sections and sections contain pages. I know, you may have never heard of sections and never created them manually. But when you create a new document, it automatically creates a section.

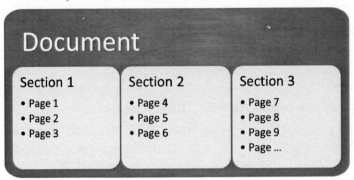

Figure 3.3 – Sections have pages

Look at the Word **status bar** at the bottom of the document. Right-click on it and choose the **Section** item. Make sure there is a tick mark next to **Section**.

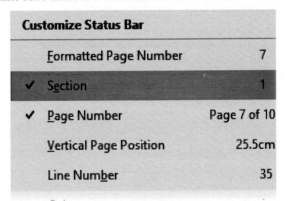

Figure 3.4 – Enabling section display from the status bar

Now, next to the page number, you can see the section number as well.

Figure 3.5 – Section number visible in the status bar

Section setup

Many things, such as headers, footers, columns, orientation, and page numbering, cannot be changed for an individual page. We need to change them at the section level. Let's take an example.

How to make a single page landscape

Say we want a wide table to be on a separate landscape page, like this:

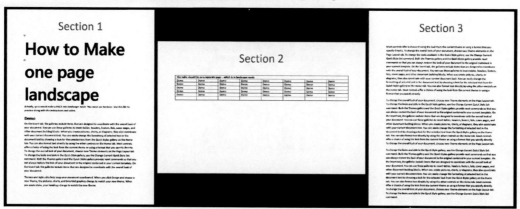

Figure 3.6 – Only one page in landscape mode

But **Layout | Orientation | Landscape** makes all pages landscape. That is not what we want. We want to make only a single page landscape. Let's see how easy it is to do this. Download this sample document and follow along with the instructions: Ch 3 - Landscape page - practice file.docx.

We cannot make a page landscape. But we *can* make a section landscape. Therefore, we need to make sure that the page with a table has its own separate section. This is done by adding a section break. Go to **Layout | Breaks | Section Breaks | Next Page** and add it before and after the table. That way, the table page is in its own section (see the status bar). Now, click on the table page and change it to landscape.

No page numbers on the title page

For professional documents (such as proposals, RFP responses, project reports, theses, and reviews), we have a title page and a table of contents, and then the actual document starts. Therefore, the document layout should be like this:

- No page numbers on the title and table of contents pages.
- Page numbering should start from the actual content.
- The page numbering should start from 1.
- The first page of the content should not show the page number.
- Show page numbers from page 2 of content onward.

Sound complicated? Watch this video and practice with the `Ch3 - Landscape page - practice file.docx` sample file:

https://hi.switchy.io/wdpn

Here are the steps involved:

1. After the title page, add a **Next Page** section break.
2. Double-click in the footer area to open the **Header & Footer** tab.
3. Unselect the **Link to Previous** option.
4. Insert page numbers. It will not start from number 1, because it is counting the physical pages.
5. To change the numbering, go to **Page Number | Format Page Numbers…** and choose **Start at 1**.

Other uses of sections

Here are some additional scenarios where using sections is the solution.

- Separate numbering for long tables of contents
- Print part of documents using separate printer trays
- Customizing the page size, margins, headers, footers, and numbering
- Adding multi-column text in between regular text.
- In short, any customization at page level is actually done at the section level.

Now, let's learn how to use tables in Word more efficiently.

Working with tables

Tables suffer from two problems. Firstly, we misuse them thoroughly. More importantly, we do not use tables at all when we really need them.

Remember one simple rule: if you are using tabs for aligning and indenting, you need to use a table.

Tables are easy to use, flexible, and completely customizable. Let's explore how you can exploit tables to your advantage.

Everything you need is there

Let's explore the power of tables. Click inside any table; you will see two tabs in the ribbon – **Table Design** and **Layout**. Everything you will ever need is there. Just notice it and use it. Remember: don't help Word; let Word help you.

The following are some common problems and quick solutions. Use the Ch3 - Word - Tables.docx file.

Table does not fit the page

This happens when you copy and paste from web pages or Excel… *do not* try to fit it yourself. That's not your job. We want to *ask* Word to fit the table on the page. How do you find the required button?

1. Click inside **Table1**.

2. Look at the tabs at the top. Tables get special tabs – **Table Design** and **Layout**. We're trying to fit a table to a page – what does that sound like, design or layout?

3. The answer is **Layout**. OK, so let's see what we have in the **Layout** tab. Read each button and think, is this button likely to help me do what I want? If not, go to the next button – you will find the answer!

4. You finally reach the **AutoFit** option. This should do the job, but autofit to what? (A page is also called a window.) Try it. Done.

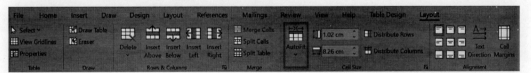

Figure 3.7 – AutoFit option

All rows need to have the same height

One row is taller than the others. We want all of them to have the same height, as shown:

Type of vehicle	Capacity
Car	5
Auto	3
Bus	30
Trailer or Double Decker	60

Type of vehicle	Capacity
Car	5
Auto	3
Bus	30
Trailer or Double Decker	60

Figure 3.8 – Distributing rows in a table

Let's find the solution:

1. Click inside **Table2**. There's no need to select the entire table. We are just informing Word that we are working with this table now.

2. Click on the **Layout** tab. Look at all the buttons and think, which one do we need? **TableRow Height**? We can use **Table Row Height**. But, you will have to change it multiple times till you find the right hight. Possible, but inefficient.

3. Next to the row height textbox, there is **Distribute Rows**. Hover the mouse cursor over it and read the tooltip. This is exactly what we want. Word will find the tallest row and adjust the height of all other rows automatically.

Just a few clicks and job done. Now, Word is helping us. Earlier, we were helping Word.

Learning more about tables

You now know that there is a button for most needs. We saw a few of them. Now, explore all the options under **Table Design** and **Layout**. You will realize how desperately you need them. You have just turned the table on tables!

Never type the same thing again – reuse it!

While writing, we may need to use something we typed earlier. That is called reuse. Word gives you so many ways to reuse things so that you never have to retype. The secret is **Quick <something>**.

I will give you an example. Let's say you are creating a new document and you need a table. You remember that there is a similar table in another document. Now, you will find and open that document. You find the table, copy and paste it, remove any unwanted portions of it, and then add data for the current document. Sound familiar?

Obviously, this is an inefficient process. Let's find an efficient method of reusing content.

Saving tables for reuse

As an example, let's use **Table3**. Suppose we sell these products often and we need to send this proposal to customers regularly.

All that we need to change is **Quantity** and **Total**. That means we can reuse this table:

1. Click on the table and go to **Layout | Select | Select Table**.
2. Go to **Insert | Table | Quick Tables | Save selection to Quick Tables Gallery…**.
3. Give it a name and save it.
4. Now, save and close the file.

You never need to open this file again to copy and paste the table.

Reusing Quick Tables

Now create a new document. How can you add the Quick Table here?

Simple. Go to **Insert | Table | Quick Tables** and choose the table you saved earlier.

This is powerful and useful. It saves time and standardizes tables.

Reusable Quick Parts

Tables are not the only thing you can reuse. Eight items in the **Insert** tab can be formatted once, saved, and reused later.

Reuse is available in the **Add to Quick <something>** menu for the following items:

- **Cover Page**
- **Table**
- **Header**
- **Footer**

- **Page Number**

- **Text Box**

- Any text (**Quick Parts**)

- **Equation**

Figure 3.9 – Eight things you can reuse in Word

The seventh item is the most powerful one. Select any text then go to **Insert | Quick Parts | Save selection to Quick Part Gallery….** Give it a name and you are ready to reuse it.

> **Exercise**
>
> Create some useful Quick Parts and start using them.

> **Notes for IT**
>
> Quick Parts data goes into a file called `BuildingBlocks.dotx`.
> This file can be centrally hosted and distributed across the organization.
> Read my blog article for details: How to deploy Office templates with
> Group Policy (efficiency365.com) (`https://efficiency365.com/2015/11/02/how-to-deploy-office-templates/`)

Your personal language coach

Microsoft Word (the Microsoft 365 version) gives intelligent suggestions beyond just spelling and grammar in the Editor. It helps you to improve your vocabulary and communicate in a professional manner. Open it from **Home | Editor**.

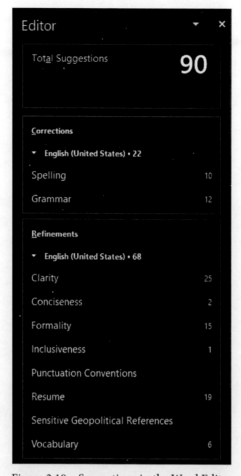

Figure 3.10 – Suggestions in the Word Editor

Not all these options may be active. Check whether they are enabled. In the desktop version, go to **File | Options | Proofing** and check the settings for spelling and grammar.

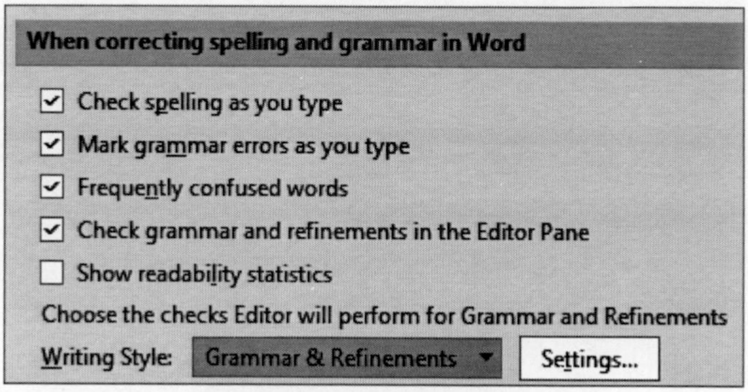

When correcting spelling and grammar in Word

- ☑ Check spelling as you type
- ☑ Mark grammar errors as you type
- ☑ Frequently confused words
- ☑ Check grammar and refinements in the Editor Pane
- ☐ Show readability statistics

Choose the checks Editor will perform for Grammar and Refinements

Writing Style: Grammar & Refinements ▼   Settings...

Figure 3.11 – Word Editor options

Scroll through this dialog and see how many amazing options are available. Not all of them may be active. Enable all the relevant ones.

This helps you with not only spelling and grammar but also many other things that matter in today's world of sophisticated communication. It helps you spot gender or racial bias, increase clarity, improve your vocabulary, reduce verbosity, and create professional content.

Look for blue dotted lines or double underlines. Here are some examples. Use the `Ch3 - Word - Editor improvements sample.docx` file to try this out:

Example	Improvement	Category
Dynamic company with young blood in sales.	new people	Inclusiveness
She is a great actress	actor	Gender Neutrality
The software is very old	incredibly old	Vocabulary
Database works on a master – slave model	primary – secondary	Sensitive references
Working from Bombay today	Mumbai	Geopolitical references

Figure 3.12 – Editor improves communication

Improving vocabulary while writing

In all versions of Word, there is a built-in thesaurus. Click on any word and press *Shift + F7*. Now you can see a pane on the right-hand side showing synonyms and antonyms. This works across all Office services – Word, Excel, PowerPoint, Outlook, and OneNote. This way, you will improve your vocabulary and refine your writing.

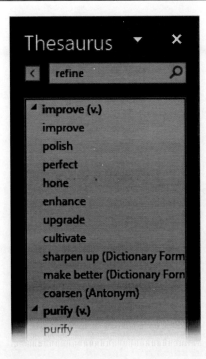

Figure 3.13 – Synonyms with Shift + F7

If you are using the Microsoft 365 version of Word, you will see a blue dotted line below some words. Right-click and see whether any of the suggested alternatives are more effective. This happens without pressing the *Shift + F7* keys.

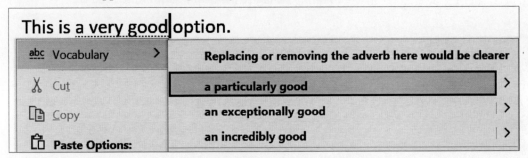

Figure 3.14 – Word Editor suggests better words

Exercise

Try this feature with a few important documents. Make a copy, look at the text, and see how you can implement this new tool.

More about Word

We have just learned about the most important parts of Word. Start using this knowledge to enhance your documents.

Of course, there is more to learn. I am confident that you will explore all the features and discover how they fit your needs.

In the next section, we will see how to create emails using Outlook.

Effective emails using Outlook

Here is the good news – what you just learned with Word will work with Outlook too. This is because Outlook uses Word as the email editor. In this section, we are going to focus only on effective email management. We will learn about time and task management in *Chapter 6, Time and Task Management*.

Using color

Using color makes your emails stand out. The usage should be subtle and professional. *Do not* add too many colors and font sizes. Outlook will then mark the email as spam.

If you have selected or created an Office theme, use that with email as well. You will get the same colors and fonts. This makes all communication from your organization look uniform and standardized. If you haven't created a theme yet, don't worry, we'll cover how to do it later in the chapter in the *Creating an Office theme for your brand* section.

Quick Parts

Minimize effort by reusing what is already there. This is similar to what we covered in the Word *Reusing Quick Parts* section we covered earlier in this chapter. Outlook also has Quick Parts for text, tables, textboxes, and equations. Word Quick Parts do not appear in Outlook. You need to create Outlook ones separately.

While writing emails, anything that looks reusable should be converted into a Quick Part.

Select it then go to **Insert | Quick Parts | Save Selection to Quick Part Gallery...** and give it a sensible name.

To insert a Quick Part into another email, go to **Insert | Quick Part** and choose the desired one from the dropdown.

Here are common uses for email Quick Parts:

- Current promotions
- Upcoming events
- Product snippets
- Disclaimers
- Links to recently published social media posts
- Recent press coverage
- A short bio
- Frequently asked questions/issues

Using tables to simplify replies

Often, we list multiple issues, queries, items, and topics of discussion in a single email. The other person has to reply by adding more paragraphs after each of your topics. It is confusing and cumbersome.

Instead, create a table with at least two columns. The first column will contain your queries, topics, issues, and so on. When replying, the other person(s) can add their responses in the second column. This is much more effective and elegant.

My thoughts/queries/issues	Your response	<person 2's response>
Is the event date finalized?		
I feel it should be a free event. What do you think?		
Should we try to get sponsors?		
The last time we did a similar event, time zones were an issue.		

Email table of contents

Reading long emails is boring and cumbersome. Make long emails more interesting and easier to read by adding a table of contents. An email is just a single long web page – there are no separate pages. So, how do we add a table of contents?

While typing the email text, apply heading styles. Outlook emails can use styles just like Word. They are not available in the **Home** tab; you must use the **Format Text** Tab ((*1*) *in Figure 3.15*), to use **Styles** (3). If the **Styles** area is inactive, check that the format is set to **HTML** (2).

It is best to add this gallery to the Quick Access Toolbar (see *Chapter 2, Components of Work*, the *Creating custom toolbars* section).

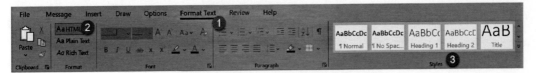

Figure 3.15 – Using styles in Outlook

Now, create the table of contents manually:

1. Go to the beginning of the email and type the headings one by one.

2. Select the heading and press *Ctrl + K* (insert link).

3. Choose **Place in This Document**. Alternatively, create the email content in Word, add the table of contents, and copy and paste it into the email.

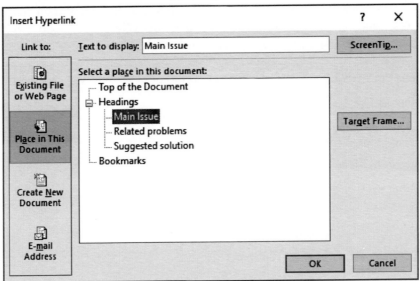

Figure 3.16 – Hyperlink within the document

The table of contents will just be hyperlinks. Here is the result. Now the reader can quickly see what you have covered in the email and jump to the desired area instantly:

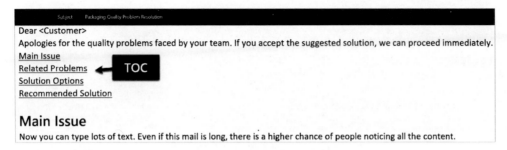

Figure 3.17 – Email table of contents

The Focused and Other folders

Outlook is smart enough to understand which emails are *important*. It moves less important emails to the **Other** folder. It learns what is important to you by analyzing your email handling patterns. As a result, 30 to 50% of emails end up in the **Other** folder – which means less manual work for you. You can just focus on the important emails in the **Focused** folder!

Less important does not mean spam or junk. We already have a separate folder for them.

Then what are *less important* emails? Here are some examples:

- Receipts
- Online shopping alerts
- Card statements
- Newsletters you have subscribed to
- Loyalty program emails
- Phone bills
- Hotel statements
- Travel notifications
- Bank statements
- Social media notifications
- Promotional emails from your subscriptions

You want to keep them for reference, but you will open them only when needed.

Sometimes, Outlook makes a mistake and an important email may end up in the **Other** folder. That is why you should go through the **Other** folder periodically. If you find an important email there, right-click on it and choose the **Always move to Focused** option.

Recent emails moved to the **Other** folder are shown just above the email list. Keep looking at the senders and notice whether any important mail is going to **Other**.

Figure 3.18 – Seeing emails in the Other folder

Not seeing the **Other** folder? Go to the **View** tab and enable this option:

Figure 3.19 – Show Focused Inbox

This option works with Microsoft mail solutions, not with third-party email providers such as Gmail or Yahoo.

Now, let's go one step further and see how to find important emails in the **Focused** inbox.

Highlighting important emails automatically

The most accurate way to know whether an email is important is to read it fully. A faster way is to see the sender and subject line – one email at a time – and then decide. This process is time consuming.

Using Outlook rules, we can save some of this time. You can ask Outlook to mark important emails in a specific color. You can then decide what exactly an important email means.

Remember, it has already filtered out less important emails and dumped them in the **Other** folder. We want to work on the **Focused** mail. The only way to do that is to check where your name is. If your name is the only name in the **To** box, that means it must be important. Make sense? So, let's create a rule:

1.   Go to **Inbox | Home | Rules | Manage Rules & Alerts…**.

2.   Go to **New Rule… | Apply rule on messages I receive**, then click on **Next**.

3. Now we need to select the condition. The **sent only to me** option is what we are looking for – which means, only my name appears in the **TO** box.

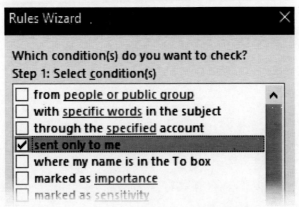

Figure 3.20 – Choosing the condition as sent only to me

4. The next step is to assign it to a category.

    At the bottom of the dialog, you must specify the category. Choosing a category applies color coding. Choose a color and rename it. We will use red and call it `High Priority`.

5. Skip the exceptions step.

6. In the last step, make sure the rule is turned on.

    Now Outlook will start looking at all incoming emails and mark them as high priority.

7. What about emails that are already in the inbox? No problem. Go to the **Rules** dialog again. Choose **Run Rules Now...** and select the rule we just created. If you have lots of emails in your inbox, this activity can take a lot of time and slow down the PC. Therefore, do it when you are not actively using the PC.

Finally, you can group by categories, so we have one group as high priority and the remaining as lower priority. Now you can handle high-priority emails first and improve email communication.

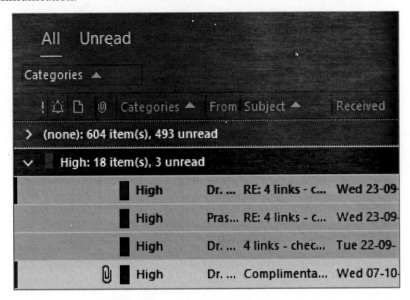

Figure 3.21 – Inbox grouped by category

You can always create more rules and add other important emails to the **High** category. For example, emails from your boss, key colleagues, important customers, and regulators can also be flagged with the **High** category. You can create 25 different categories to color code emails, tasks, meetings, and contacts.

Some emails, such as subscriptions, will have you as the only name in the **To** list. But those may not be important at all. We can always add exceptions to our Outlook rules to handle those cases.

Taking notes using OneNote

If you capture notes during meetings, research, or studies, you must explore OneNote. There are hundreds of note-taking applications. Still, trust me, you need OneNote.

Why do you need OneNote?

Word, Excel, and PowerPoint are used for creating formal documents, spreadsheets, and presentations. For everything else, use OneNote.

Business users can link notes to meetings. Whether you take notes on your laptop, mobile, or paper, you can still link them to meetings in the calendar. This alone is enough justification to use OneNote.

OneNote is an unlimited supply of electronic diaries. In OneNote, these are called notebooks. If you carry a paper notepad or diary, you can carry only one at a time. The problem is, in a single diary, multiple topics get mixed up. Even if you have a tabbed organizer diary, there is a limit to how many pages you can insert there. Sooner or later, you will need a new organizer.

How to get OneNote

Quite often, you may not find OneNote on your PC. No problem. There are two ways to install it:

- If your IT team manages your PC, ask them to install it.
- Else, go to https://onenote.com/download and install it.

OneNote has two versions for PC – desktop and the Windows 10 version. Install the desktop version of OneNote. In this book, all instructions and screenshots are from the desktop version. Remember to install OneNote on your mobile phones as well. OneNote is free to use on PC, Mac, browsers, iOS, and Android.

Adding notebooks to OneNote

OneNote installation creates one default notebook. That is more like a help file. Read it and then leave it alone. Create as many notebooks as you need. To start with, create at least one new notebook for learning purposes and then add more as needed.

Go to **File | New | Create Notebook**. Make sure you create the notebook on OneDrive. That way, you can sync the notebooks across all your devices automatically.

In each OneNote notebook, you can separate topics using any number of sections. Within each section, you can have an unlimited supply of pages. OneNote pages have no width or length constraint – you can expand them as needed.

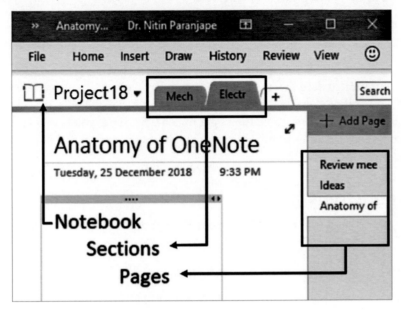

Figure 3.22 – OneNote notebook structure

Mobile to desktop sync

Make sure you log in using the same account on all devices. Open the notebook on mobile once. That way, all changes will sync automatically across all devices. If all devices are online, the sync takes just a few seconds. If a device is offline, it will sync when an internet connection becomes available.

Myth – a stylus/pen is a must to use OneNote

Some think that a stylus or pen is essential if using OneNote. Absolutely not. OneNote can be used with just the keyboard on a PC/Mac. You can also use the mouse for drawing. On the mobile app, use your finger to scribble notes. It converts handwriting to text quite accurately – even if done using a finger, without a stylus. The AI logic improves over time. Here is an example:

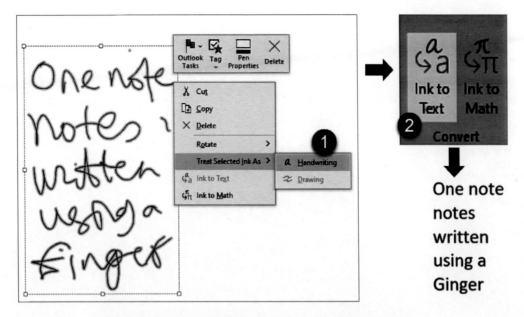

Figure 3.23 – Converting handwritten notes to text in OneNote

I wrote this on mobile using my finger. Let your notebook synchronize with the desktop, then do the following:

1. Select your text using **Draw | Lasso tool**.

2. Right-click and choose **Treat Selected Ink As | Handwriting**.

3. Now go to **Draw | Ink to Text**. That is it!

Of course, in my example, I wrote the F so badly it thought it was a G… my bad.

Autosaving – no folders or filenames

OneNote saves everything automatically. Once saved, it will synchronize across all devices. There is no need to save manually. That way, you do not have to worry about folder and filenames.

If you want to find something, use *Ctrl + F* to find it on the current page and *Ctrl + E* to find it across notebooks. This is simple, elegant, and effective.

Linking notes to meetings

We have been taking notes during meetings and lectures for decades. Can you find those notes after, say, 6 months easily? Usually, you forget which filename it was saved as, which notepad, or which page. OneNote solves all these problems in a smart way.

For this to work, the meeting must be in your Outlook calendar. Now, you can link notes – whether you capture them using OneNote on desktop, the OneNote mobile app, or on a paper notepad. Let's see how to link notes to meetings.

Linking notes to meetings on a desktop PC

To do so, take the following steps:

1. Go to Outlook Calendar and find the meeting.

2. Right-click on the meeting and choose **Meeting Notes**.

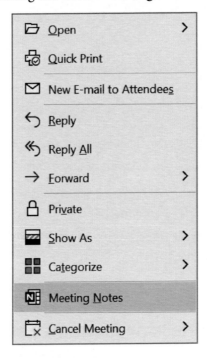

Figure 3.24 – Linking notes to a Calendar meeting

3. Choose **Take notes on your own.**

4. Select the correct OneNote notebook and section.

    OneNote will open with a new page. This will *not* be a blank page. It will contain all the details of the meeting.

5. Type your meeting notes on this page.

6. If you want to send this notes page to meeting attendees, go to **Home | Email Page**.

7. When the meeting is over, nothing has to be done, as it is on **AutoSave**.

How can you find these notes after some time? Well, that is simple:

1. Go to Outlook Calendar and find the meeting.

2. Right-click on it and choose the same **Meeting Notes** option.

3. Choose **Take notes on your own**.

Now, Outlook will find the exact notes page in OneNote and open it automatically. Simple, useful, and efficient!

Linking notes captured on a mobile phone

Nowadays, people only take their mobile to meetings and capture notes using their favorite mobile app. Let's see how to link these notes to meetings.

The Outlook mobile app does not have the ability to link meetings with notes. Not to worry. We will use the OneNote mobile app:

1. Start the OneNote mobile app. Choose a notebook and add a new page. You cannot link Sticky Notes to meetings.

2. Capture notes by typing or writing using your finger or stylus.

    At this stage, there is no meeting linked to this page.

3. Later, when you open your laptop/PC, this OneNote page will sync automatically.

4. Open the same page on the desktop.

5. From the **Home** tab, choose **Meeting Details**.

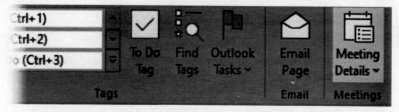

Figure 3.25 – The Meeting Details tab

6. Choose the corresponding meeting.

This is how you link a page to a meeting retroactively.

Linking notes written in a notepad or diary

Well, there is no technology involved here! Just a pen/pencil and paper. No problem. Follow these steps:

1.   Write your notes on paper as usual.

2.   After the meeting, open the OneNote mobile app.

3.   Add a new page.

4.   Capture photos of the paper notes on that page.

5.   Let the page sync with desktop.

6.   Now, open the same page on desktop. Use **Home | Meeting Details** and choose the appropriate meeting.

7.   OneNote will now add all the details of the meeting and link the page to the meeting. to link it to the desired meeting. Done!

Searching for text in scanned documents and photos

This feature is available only in the desktop version of OneNote.

You can search in any scanned document using OneNote. The document can be in any format, but usually it will be in PDF format:

1.   Open the PDF using any PDF reader app.

2.   Go to **File | Print | Send to OneNote**.

3.   Choose the notebook and section.

     Now all the scanned pages will go into a single OneNote page.

4.   Alternatively, add a blank page in OneNote and choose **Insert | File Printout**.

     Now all the scanned pages are added as images to the OneNote page.

5.   On that OneNote page, press *Ctrl + F* and type the word you want to find.

This works on OneNote desktop, Mac, and mobile versions but not on Windows 10 and browser versions. Enjoy.

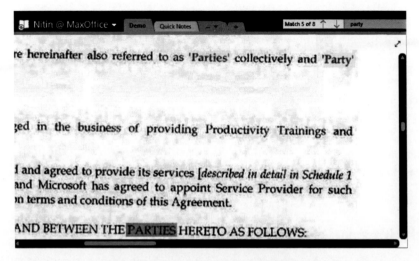

Figure 3.26 – Searching in scanned documents

There is more. Right-click on a scanned page image and choose **Copy text from (one or all pages)** or **Image**. Now you can paste the recognized text anywhere and edit it. This amazing feature has been available for the last 15 years! Imagine…

OneNote calculator

Just type a mathematical expression in OneNote and press = and the spacebar. OneNote will give you the results instantly. Here are some examples:

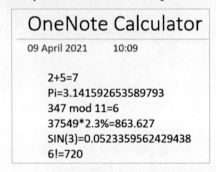

Figure 3.27 – OneNote calculation examples

Now that you know the power of OneNote, start using it and explore more, such as the following:

- Insert audio (or video) recordings of meetings and link the audio to notes.
- Insert any objects, create tags and search for them, create templates and reuse them, and solve math equations.

- You can also add OneNote to Teams and capture shared notes as we will see in (*Chapter 7, Efficient Teamwork and Meetings*).

> **Exercise**
>
> Create at least two notebooks and save them in OneDrive. Start taking notes using OneNote.

Now, you can capture notes more effectively. But what if you are presenting? In the next section, we will see how to create and deliver presentations effectively and with high impact.

Flowcharts with Visio

Do you create flowcharts and process diagrams by assembling shapes from PowerPoint? If yes, stop doing it. Start using Visio. Since September 2021, a powerful diagramming tool, Visio, is a part of Office and Microsoft 365 commercial licenses (`https://www.microsoft.com/en-us/microsoft-365/blog/2021/06/09/bringing-visio-to-microsoft-365-diagramming-for-everyone`).

Go to `Office.com` and then **All Apps**. Look for the Visio icon. This is the lite, web version.

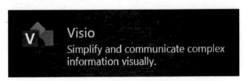

Figure 3.28 – Using Visio for flowcharting

Explore the available templates for diagrams, flowcharts, process diagrams, business matrices, Venn diagrams, cycle diagrams, and pyramid diagrams.

Let's create a flowchart to get going with Visio. Choose **Basic Flowchart** from the templates and click **Create**. On the left side, you have a collection of shapes (also called stencils). There are 12 collections, which include **Basic Shapes**, **Flowchart Shapes**, **Cycle Diagram shapes**, **Matrix Diagram shapes**, **Callouts**, **Arrows**, **Process Shapes**, **Banners**, **Pyramid shapes**, **Venn diagram shapes**, **Math shapes**, and **Symbols**. You can open and use multiple shape stencils, as required.

Select a shape and drag it onto the page. Hover the mouse cursor over the shape. You can do two things: connect it to another existing shape by dragging the connection handles (green hollow circles around the shape) or click any of the arrows to choose another shape and automatically connect to it.

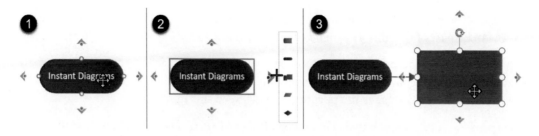

Figure 3.29 – Selecting and connecting shapes

Try this out. Once you get the hang of it, you can create complex diagrams very quickly. Right-click each shape to customize it or change it.

Add shapes, connect them, and create a diagram. Explore the themes and colors. Click the **Design** tab and change the diagram layout as required.

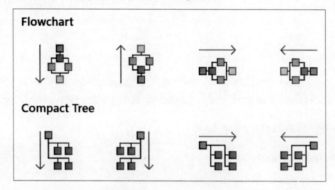

Figure 3.30 – Visio layouts

Like all Office apps, multiple people can edit the same diagram together. You can save it as a Visio file (VSDX) or export it as an image or PDF. You can also copy and paste the diagram to other apps, such as PowerPoint.

Unlike PowerPoint, diagrams in Visio need to be built one shape at a time. The premium version of Visio can connect to a database and create diagrams automatically. Using this feature, you can create complex organization charts instantly. It can also create a workflow and then export it to Power Automate (*Chapter 8, Automating Work without Programming*).

High-impact presentations with PowerPoint

Word and Excel have precise outputs. You know when the document or report is complete. PowerPoint has no endpoint. People spend hours (even years) refining their presentations and still – the outcome is poor!

The majority of presentations are boring and longer than necessary. In this section, we will see how to be part of the minority – and that too without spending too much effort.

Each presentation has a purpose. The purpose could be selling, teaching, convincing, explaining, discussing, brainstorming, reviewing, and so on. The idea is to present your "*point*" with "*power*" to achieve the purpose. Always keep this in mind.

People praising your presentation is not enough; it should also achieve the purpose with minimal effort.

> **Note**
> Make sure you have the Microsoft 365 version of PowerPoint installed on the desktop PC. Many options in this section will *not* work with the browser or *desktop-only* versions of PowerPoint, such as 2016, 2019, and 2021 – even if it is the latest version.

Design Ideas

In most presentations, the first slide is important – because most people see it for the longest duration. Therefore, the first slide should be really attention grabbing.

Let's ask PowerPoint to create one for you:

1. Create a new blank presentation.

2. On the first slide, put the title of your presentation.

    Don't put a long title – put one or two relevant words. For example, in this case, I typed `Healthcare`.

3. Click the **Design Ideas** button in the **Home** tab.

    Now, PowerPoint will use sophisticated AI and show many options for the slide. These options appear in a separate pane on the right side.

    Usually, the first item is a video and the rest of them are pictures.

4. Try it out. In most cases, it gives you amazing-looking slides in just a few clicks.

Here are some examples of design ideas for the first slide of a new presentation:

Figure 3.31 – Design Ideas

Design Ideas creates a template with colors, fonts, and layouts that match the visual on the first slide. This way, your entire presentation looks professional.

All kinds of slides can use Design Ideas. It works with bullets, pictures, timelines, and SmartArt. Download this sample presentation to have a look at what is possible with Design Ideas. Use this file to practice with Design Ideas:

```
Ch3 - PowerPoint - Design Ideas Samples.pptx
```

> **Exercise**
>
> Look at your existing presentations. Make sure the first slide is based upon a high-impact design idea.
>
> Revisit every slide and see which ones can be improved with Design Ideas. Always create a copy of the slide or presentation before trying anything new.

Design templates

Design Ideas creates a matching template when you use it on the first slide of a new presentation.

Otherwise, you can use design templates to control the colors, fonts, and layouts across the presentation. These are available in the **Design** tab. Choose the design early. If you apply a different design template to an existing presentation, many slides could be disturbed. You need to cross-check each slide and repair it as needed.

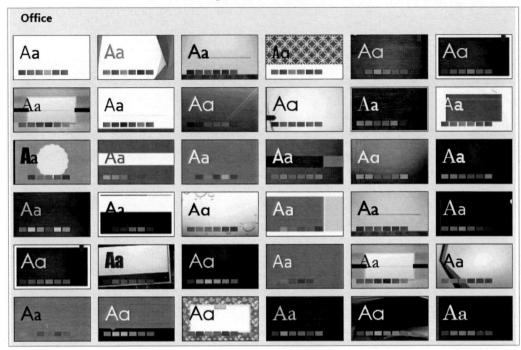

Figure 3.32 – Design templates

Organizations often create their own custom design templates that incorporate their corporate branding guidelines.

Stock images

We spend an enormous amount of time finding clipart and images to enhance our slides. Randomly inserting images from the internet is risky. It is illegal and unfair to use images that are someone else's copyright without permission.

That is why PowerPoint has an ever-growing collection of stock images and art. **Insert | Pictures | Stock Images…** is a good place to start. But there is more. All these are free to use in Office apps:

Figure 3.33 – Picking up stock images

Actively explore these collections when you have time. Knowing what is available is also part of learning. You do not need to see each picture or sticker, but at least click on each category and see what is available.

All videos are short (a few seconds) and designed to loop. When you add a video to a slide, it will run automatically when the slide is visible and will repeat until the slide is no longer in view. Of course, you can change this behavior from the **Playback** tab.

Make sure that you explore **Insert | 3D Models | Stock 3D Models…**. These can add instant impact. You can animate them and rotate/move them during the presentation.

Design Ideas uses visuals/icons from these stock images to create slides for you.

SmartArt

Here is another example of less effort–more impact. You just type bullets and PowerPoint will create a diagram for you. There is only one problem. Which is the most suitable diagram? That *you* must decide.

How do you decide? Well, just look at all the available diagrams once. There are 145 of them.

Do not get stressed. It will just take 20 minutes of your time. But it will deliver lifelong benefits! Go to **Insert | SmartArt** to open the dialog. Now follow the steps:

1. On the left side, there are various categories of diagrams.
2. Click on each category.
3. Now, click on each diagram.
4. Look at the bigger diagram and think "Where can I use it?"

5. Read the first sentence from the description that displays below. It tells you *when* to use this diagram. Do this for all diagrams and you are ready.

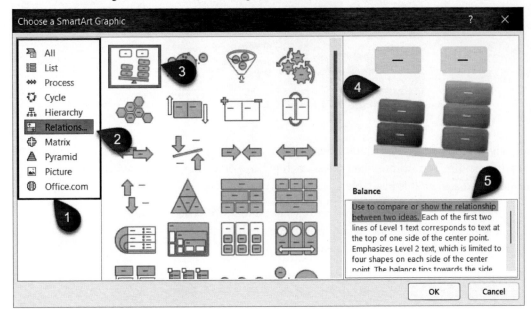

Figure 3.34 – Learning how to use SmartArt

You just built a visual vocabulary. You do not have to try and remember all 145 diagrams. Your brain is extremely good at remembering visual things. Next time you need a diagram, your brain will help you find the right one. It becomes easier with more usage.

Insert the right diagram and then type text to build it. Each diagram uses text differently. The sample text given shows how the diagram uses text.

Once you create a diagram, you will see the **SmartArt Design** tab. Here, you can change colors across the diagram and change the look and feel using styles.

Download this presentation that shows base text and a diagram. Use it to learn about the effective use of SmartArt:

`Ch3 - PowerPoint - SmartArt samples.pptx`

Design Ideas often uses SmartArt along with icons to convert text slides into compelling visuals.

> **Exercise**
>
> Make a copy of a recent presentation. Look at each slide and see where SmartArt can replace existing text or manually created diagrams.

Layouts

When you add a new slide, two textboxes appear automatically. That is the layout. Often, what you want to show in the slide does not match the current layout. Then, you delete the textboxes (the technical name is placeholders) and manually add pictures, text, and so on.

This is the most inefficient way of using PowerPoint.

The correct way is to first choose the correct layout and then add content inside it.

All of us know two layouts. The title layout appears for the first slide of a new presentation. Title and content is the layout for the rest of the slides. But there are more layouts available.

Open the **New Slide** dropdown and choose a layout.

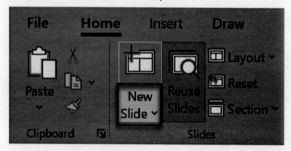

Figure 3.35 – Choosing the layout while creating a new slide

If you click on the upper part of the **New Slide** button, it will choose the layout automatically. If you open the dropdown, you can choose the layout you need.

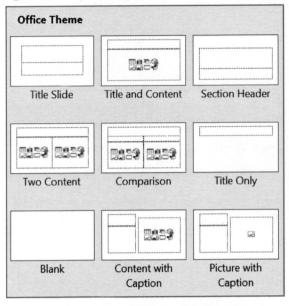

Figure 3.36 – Choosing a slide layout

You can create your own layouts as well. Go to **View | Slide Master**. This will show the layout that the current slide is using. Right-click on the layout to duplicate it and rename it. Now change the layout as per your needs.

One common way to customize the layout is to have a title and four charts or pictures. Another way is to add company logos to the main slide master so that it appears on all slides.

Capturing screenshots

The Snip & Sketch tool in Windows is popular for capturing screenshots. However, PowerPoint (and Word, Excel, Outlook, and OneNote) has a simpler method available to capture screenshots directly.

Go to **Insert** (1) | **Screenshot** (2). Choose the screen or choose **Screen Clipping**.

If you choose **Screen Clipping** (3), PowerPoint itself will disappear. The window behind PowerPoint will now be visible with the selection cursor (like the Snip tool).

Select the required area. The screenshot is now a part of the slide. Simple and effective. Try it out. Before choosing **Screenshot**, use *Alt + Tab* to make sure that the desired window is behind PowerPoint.

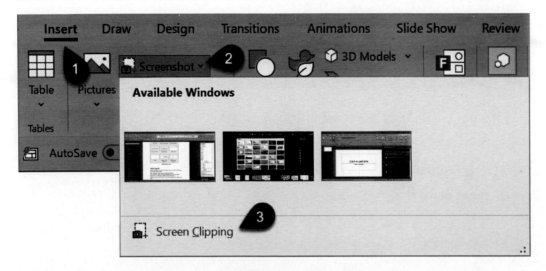

Figure 3.37 – Adding screenshots to your presentation

Also remember that you can insert a video recording of screen activity as well using **Insert | Screen Recording**. The recorded screen video becomes a video in the current slide. You can save it as an MP4 file as well. Just right-click on the video and choose **Save Media as…**.

Animation, transitions, and Morph

By default, when you present a slide, all items on it are visible. If you want to change this, you need to use animation. Animation works *within* a slide. If you want to do something *across* two slides – such as adding a page turn effect, for example – you use transitions.

One extremely powerful transition is Morph. It can create amazing visual effects with minimal effort. Animation and Morph are visual concepts. The best way to learn is by seeing it. Watch this video twice. The first time, just watch it. The second time, open the `Ch 3 - PowerPoint - Animation Samples.pptx` file and try it out:

https://hi.switchy.io/f33

Remember to use animation and Morph only when it adds value to the topic/subject you are covering. *Do not* use them just because they are there.

> **Warning**
>
> If you are presenting online, minimize the use of animation and Morph. Moving images do not render well in online meetings.

Creating videos and GIFs

Once the presentation is ready, you can add voice narration, webcam video (a talking head), annotation, and laser pointer gestures to it. Finally, you can convert it to a proper MP4 video and share it with others or upload it to YouTube (or other streaming services). To do so, take the following steps:

1. Go to **Slide Show | Record Slide Show**.

2. Enable webcam and choose the correct mic.

3. Click the record button. For each slide, you can talk, annotate the slide with drawings, use a pointer, and move to the next slide.

    When you finish, all the audio, annotations, and webcam footage become part of the base presentation. It also adds timing for each slide – depending on how long you spoke on it.

4. Now, go to **File | Export | Video** and choose a resolution.

Your MP4 is ready!

You can also use the option **File |Export – Create an Animated GIF**. Select the slides, decide the resolution and whether to include the slide background and then click the **Create GIF** button. That's it. Now the animated GIF will run in any browser or social media platform.

Coach

We rarely have the luxury of a presentation expert coaching us. Most of us learn how to present by trial and error. Now, using AI, PowerPoint can help you improve your presentation skills. Try this with a smaller presentation first:

1. Make sure you are connected to the internet.

2. Open a presentation that you want to rehearse.

3. Go to the **Slide Show** tab | **Rehearse with Coach**. If you do not see this button on PowerPoint desktop, open the presentation in a browser.

4. Allow PowerPoint to use the microphone. Choose **Start**.

5. Deliver the presentation as you normally would.

6. PowerPoint may give suggestions during the presentation as well.

7. When you finish, you will get a summary of all the areas for improvement.

8. Improve those areas and rehearse again.

The final report looks like this. The exact recommendations will be specific to your content:

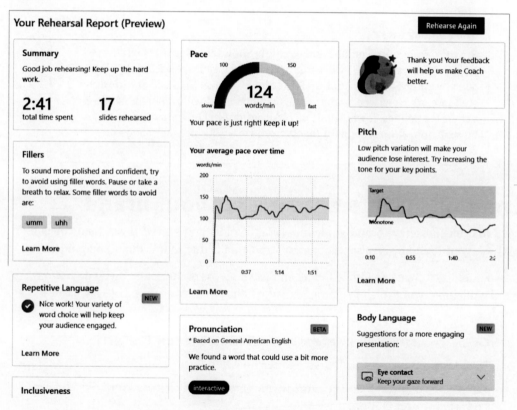

Figure 3.38 – PowerPoint Coach results

Exercise

Make a copy of a recent presentation. Go through each slide and see how you can enhance it using Design Ideas, SmartArt, layouts, and stock images. Compare before and after. Learn and apply.

What if we want to send a presentation as read-only? Why not convert it to a web page and share the link? This is done using Sway, which we will cover in a later section of this chapter.

Now that you know how to create documents and presentations efficiently, it is time to put all this knowledge into practice. There are two ways to do this. For new documents that you create, you already know how to do it properly. But you can also open recent old documents and refine them. That will help you practice these new skills and learn better.

All your documents and presentations should be branded, professional, and uniform. To ensure this, you can create your own Office theme and standardize it across your organization, which is what we'll cover in the next section.

Self-Running Kiosk

Pro tip: Create a presentation and use **Slide Show tab | Record Narration** to add audio narration. This will automatically add timings to each slide. Now, go to the **Slide Show** tab | **Set Up Slide Show**. Choose **Browsed at a kiosk (full screen)**. Now, when you run the presentation, it will run on its own as per the set timings. It will ignore any touches/clicks. Only *Esc* can stop the presentation. This is useful for touchscreen kiosks during trade shows or conferences.

Creating an Office theme for your brand

Does your business have brand guidelines (brand colors and fonts)? If yes, then you can reinforce your brand by creating documents and emails that follow the brand guidelines.

The solution is to create an Office theme and use it across documents. If you do not have brand guidelines, you can choose from existing Office themes as well. Let's try it out in Word:

1. Open a document with styles and choose **Themes** from the **Design** tab.

2. Hover the mouse over each theme to see how it looks.

3. Choose the one you like. The same themes are available across Word, Excel, PowerPoint, and Outlook.

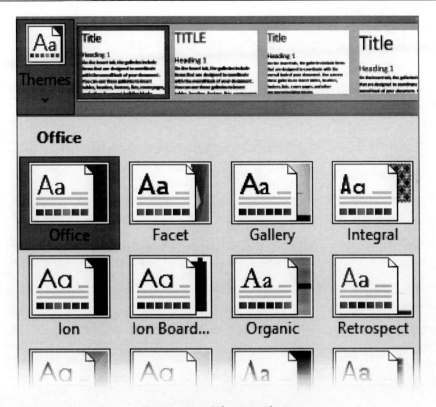

Figure 3.39 – Selecting a theme

Want to create a theme of your own? No problem. Choose the colors and fonts:

1. Go to the **Design** tab, open the **Colors** dropdown, and choose **Customize Colors…**.

2. There are 10 colors. Change them to create a custom palette.

Choose your colors and fonts wisely. If you do not understand graphic design, choose matching colors using sites such as Adobe Color - https://color.adobe.com/create or Paletton - https://paletton.com/.

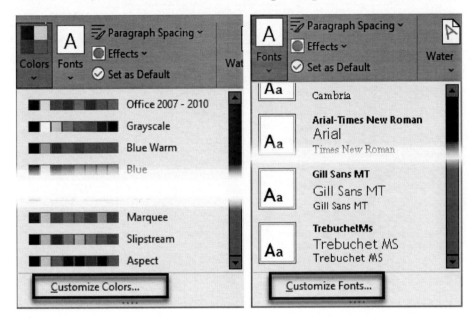

Figure 3.40 – Customizing colors and fonts

3.   Next, from the **Design | Fonts | Customize Fonts…** option, choose two fonts – one for headings and one for the body. Choose fonts that come bundled with Windows 10.

     If you send a presentation using uncommon fonts to others, it may not render correctly. The solution? Embed the fonts. Go to **File | Options | Save** and choose **Embed fonts in the file**. The side effect is that the file size will increase.

4.   Once you are happy with the look and feel, go to **Design | Themes | Save Current Theme…**. Give it a name and save it. The file extension is THMX.

How do you apply this new theme to any document? Open the document. Then, open the **Themes** dropdown, as shown previously, choose **Browse for Themes…**, and select the template. That is it.

Choosing the right color palette and fonts requires knowledge of graphic design. It is an art. If you are creating a brand template, it is better to seek help from a graphic design expert or agency.

Now, let's switch gears and look at one of the most common activities – copy and pasting.

Efficient copy and pasting

The *second* most used keyboard shortcut is *Ctrl + C*. The *most common*, unfortunately, is undo – *Ctrl + Z*. Often, the reason you need to undo is that a copy-and-paste action did not work as expected. The solution is to understand the right way to copy and paste.

The "right" way to copy and paste

Copying is easy. Select the content, right-click, and choose **Copy** (*Ctrl + C*). The content goes to the clipboard. While pasting, you can choose from different formats. If you go to the destination and paste (*Ctrl + V*), the default format is used. The default may not be the format you were expecting.

When we paste content, we have to answer two questions: where exactly do we want to paste and which format do we want to paste in? Both these questions can be answered in a simple way. Go to the desired destination (slide, paragraph, cell, and so on) and right-click. Now, all the available paste formats are shown. Hover the mouse cursor over them to see how it will paste. Click when you reach the desired format.

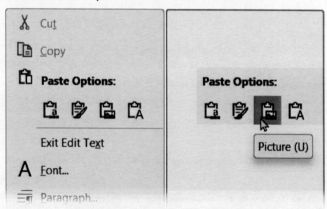

Figure 3.41 – Choosing a paste option

The exact set of options that appear here will depend on what you are pasting and where. But usually, the options are **Keep Source Formatting (K)**, **Match Merge Formatting (M)**, **Picture (U)**, and **Keep Text Only (T)**. Usually, each option has a shortcut key. If you know the key, just type it. There's no need to select it with the mouse.

Therefore, the new way of copy and pasting is as follows:

1. Copy from the source.
2. Right-click at the destination.
3. Choose the desired format.

This concept works across all Microsoft Office tools. Try it out and see how simple, efficient, and predictable the copy-and-paste process becomes.

What if you forgot to right-click and choose? No problem. Microsoft knows that you will forget.

Stop. Do not undo.

Look at the icon that appears on its own. Click on it. All the paste options are still available.

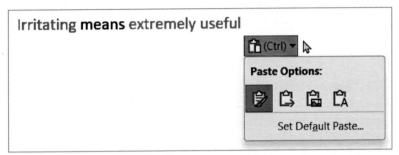

Figure 3.42 – Irritating means useful!

Everyone gets irritated with this icon. But it is an invaluable "afterthought menu." Use it to your advantage. Press and release the *Ctrl* key to open the menu. Then, take a pause for a second and press the relevant shortcut key (for example, **Text** is **T**).

> Do you end up using the same formatting option repeatedly? No problem. With Word, OneNote, and Outlook, you can set the default paste option. Remember, Any feature that is irritating must be extremely useful.
>
> Why? Because Microsoft also knows that people get irritated with it. Despite that, they decided to keep it. They are taking a risk of customer dissatisfaction to keep the feature. That means it must be really adding some significant value to humanity. It is our job to find the benefit it offers.
>
> The "afterthought menu" is the best example of this concept. Other examples include the GetPivotData function in Excel, meetings appearing as a chat in Teams, and the chart color changing when pasted into PowerPoint.

Paste and link

Usually, when you copy content from a source and paste it somewhere else, it does not change when the source changes. If you want it to change, you need to paste and link. This is done by choosing **Paste Special**. Go to **Home** | **Paste** | **Paste Special...**.

> **Remember This Shortcut**
> The shortcut for **Paste Special** is *Ctrl + Alt + V*.

This opens the **Paste Special** dialog. The exact options that appear in this dialog will change depending on the type of content in the clipboard. In most cases, at least with Microsoft Office apps, you can choose the **Paste link** option. The available formats will change. Choose the one you want.

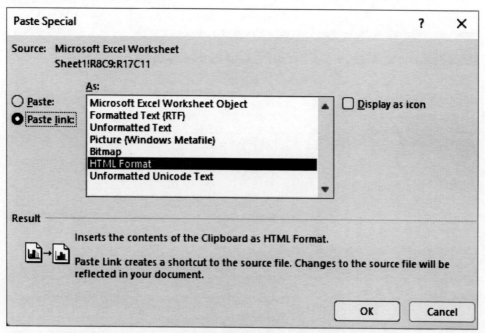

Figure 3.43 – Paste link in Word from Excel

The pasted content remembers its origin. Now you can close the source file and the destination file. When the destination file opens the next time, it will try to find the source file and update itself.

Paste link works across all Office apps. It may also work with some non-Microsoft apps. If the source file is not found, you will see a message. You can relocate the file and re-establish the link.

Links can break if files are renamed, moved across drives, or uploaded to the cloud. It is always safer to check all links in the **File | Info | Edit Links to Files** dialog. The **Edit Links to Files** option is visible below the file properties. This option is visible only if the file has any external linkages. Select all links and choose **Check Status**. Resolve any errors or mismatched file locations.

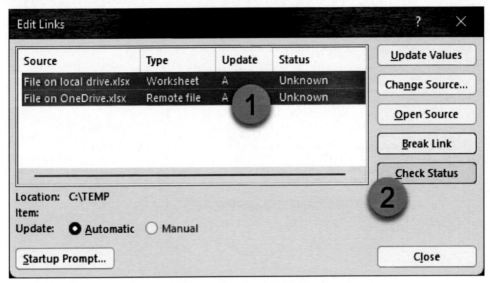

Figure 3.44 – Edit Links – Check Status

> **A Word of Caution**
>
> When you send a file with linked content to others, they will most likely not have access to the source file. If you don't want the target audience to get confused with link errors, it is a good idea to break the links. Make a copy of the file. Go to **File | Info | Edit Links to Files**. Select all links and choose **Break Links**. This will remove the link but keep the pasted data.

Moving paragraphs

When we want to reorder paragraphs, most of us will select and cut and paste. There is a delightfully more efficient way of doing this. Just click inside the paragraph and use the following keyboard shortcut:

Shift + Alt + Up arrow or *Down arrow*

Try it out. Aren't you wondering **WDINKTE (why did I not know this earlier)**?!

The delight is doubled when you realize that this is the fastest way of reordering rows in a table (Word only, not PowerPoint).

This shortcut works whenever there is a paragraph context. Remember to also use it in the SmartArt editor to rearrange diagram items instantly. It does not work in Excel because there are no paragraphs.

Converting any content into a picture

Anything you copy goes to the clipboard, as we have seen in *Chapter 2, Components of Work*, in the *Efficiency Primer – Get 24 Clipboards* section. Do you want to convert it into a picture? Right-click in any Office app and choose **Picture (U)** from **Paste Options**. Right-click on the picture and choose **Save as Picture** to save it as a PNG, JPG, SVG, GIF, TIF, or BMP.

This is a very handy way of converting anything into a picture. This is very useful in PowerPoint.

Chart color changes after pasting

When you copy a chart from Excel to PowerPoint, the colors change. The solution? Look at the "afterthought menu" that appears after you paste the chart. Choose the **Keep Source Formatting & Link Data (F)** option.

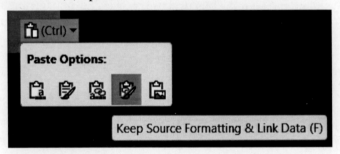

Figure 3.45 – Keeping source formatting in charts

Please note that a chart pasted into PowerPoint from Excel is linked by default. You do not have to choose the **Paste link** option.

Next, let's look at one powerful tool using which you can create web pages – without knowing programming: Sway.

Instant web pages using Sway

Sway is an amazingly simple but powerful tool. Sway creates web pages. You do not need to learn or understand any programming, HTML, or JavaScript. You just supply the content. Sway will design, create, and publish the web page instantly and give you sharing links. It is that simple.

Figure 3.46 – Creating a sway

Sway is a browser-only app. Log in to the Office home page. Go to **All Apps** and choose **Sway**.

Figure 3.47 – Sway icon

Start from a blank page or use existing templates. Just scroll through the available templates and you will understand the practical use of Sway. Event pages, newsletters, presentations, FAQs, help manuals, product pages, circulars, notices, price lists, and a lot more scenarios are applicable.

Adding content

Go to **Storyline** and add a title. After that, you can add headings, regular text, images, audio, video, embedded content, and so on. Create a sample page and practice adding different content types.

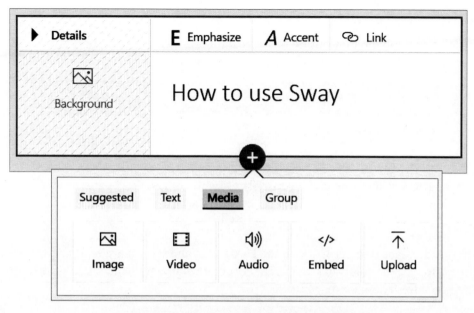

Figure 3.48 – Adding content and getting a web page

Select multiple pictures and group them. Try different group types. The **Stack** group type is ideally suited to show multiple photos.

Figure 3.49 – Stacked images in Sway

Playing and testing

At any point, click on the **Play** button to see how the sway looks. Sway pages are visible on any browser. The page adjusts to the screen size automatically.

Figure 3.50 – Playing a sway

Navigate by scrolling horizontally or vertically using the mouse, keyboard, or touch.

Designing

Sway has ready-made designs. Click on the **Design** tab and try out available styles. You can also customize the colors based on your corporate brand guidelines. Click the **Remix!** button to get a fresh design every time.

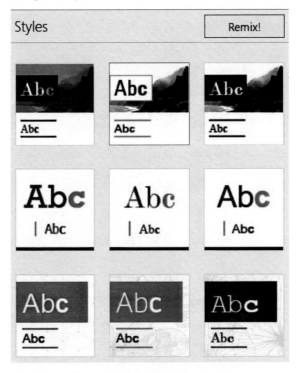

Figure 3.51 – Sway design styles

Publishing

Once you are happy with the design, click the **Share** button. Two types of links are available:

- One for your internal company staff – they have to log in to see the page.
- You can create an anonymous link that anyone in the world can view.

Be careful not to add confidential or sensitive data to publicly available Sway pages.

You can also get a QR code that you can add to websites, media campaigns, or printed communication.

Figure 3.52 – Sway sharing options

Creating a Sway page from Word

Creating a Sway page from Word is easy to do. First, you have to make sure you have used styles in the Word document:

1. From the **File** tab, choose **Transform**.
2. Choose the style and click the **Transform** button.

3. Now you get a Sway web page instantly – with proper navigation and a table of contents. Get the link and share it. Simple, is it not?

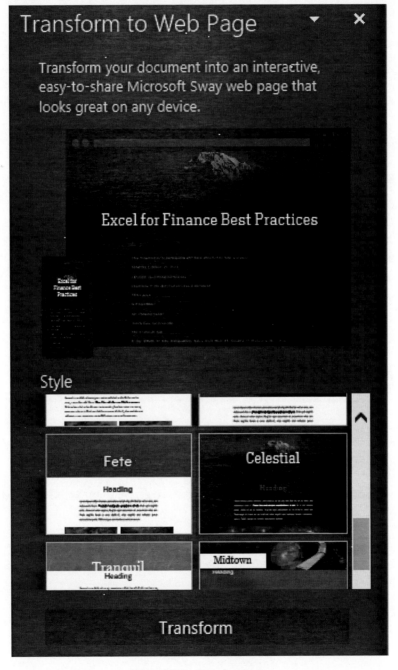

Figure 3.53 – Word to Sway

Creating a Sway page from PowerPoint

Creating a Sway page from PowerPoint can also be done easily:

1. Go to the Sway home page.
2. Choose **Start from a document**.
3. Choose a PowerPoint presentation.

Again, you get a nice Sway page with a table of contents. Change the design if needed and share. Simple and efficient!

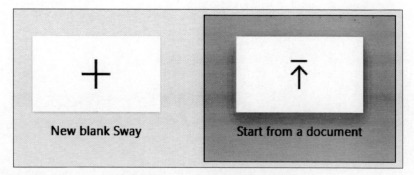

Figure 3.54 – Sway from PowerPoint

Summary

In this chapter, we learned how to create content efficiently. More importantly, we saw the underlying principles of efficiency helping us across all apps.

This is not the end point. It is just the beginning. I hope you now realize that every need has a corresponding feature. It is in our interest to explore and discover.

In the next chapter, we will focus on data: how to get data, clean it, analyze it, and present it – all this with minimal effort and maximum impact.

4
Intelligent Data Analysis

Now that we know how to manage documents efficiently, let's think about managing data. With documents, we have content and formatting. Here, we have data gathering, data cleanup, and analysis. We should not waste time and effort on cleanup; rather, we should focus all our energy on effective analysis. Let's start with a simple question – what exactly is analysis?

Analysis means trying to learn all possible useful things from the data, and then using that knowledge to take actions that can improve the future.

This simple but powerful definition will help you to learn and use Excel, Power BI, and any other data analysis tool efficiently.

In this chapter, we will learn about four apps: Lists, Forms, Excel, and Power BI.

The following table depicts the specific purpose of these apps:

Purpose	App
Capture data from multiple persons.	Lists
Conduct surveys, polls, or quizzes.	Forms
Enter data, cleanup, analysis, charts, dashboards, reports, and **MIS** (short for **Management Information System**)	Excel and Power BI
Dashboards, interactive reports, AI analysis.	Excel and Power BI

Technical requirements

The sample files used in this chapter are available here in the `Chapter 04` folder: `https://static.packt-cdn.com/downloads/978-1-80107-226-7_ExerciseFiles.zip`

Data analysis in three steps

There are three steps involved:

1. Get the data.
2. Clean it up.
3. Analyze it (and then act on it).

Obviously, analysis (and action) is the crucial step.

Unfortunately, we spend too much time cleaning up the data, as mentioned in *step 2*.

Why does the data need cleaning? Because we do not understand how exactly to get data in the first step! It is a bad, vicious cycle.

Figure 4.1 – Data analysis process

Let's solve the problem in a simple, logical manner.

When you buy products, or log in to an app and use it, or get a medical test done, or just travel to a place – all these activities are generating data. Someone is typing it somewhere in an app. In other cases, data can be generated automatically, such as a history of which videos you have seen. All this is **input data**.

Input data is usually lengthy as it has an ever-growing number of rows. By looking at and scrolling the input data, we cannot learn useful things.

To learn usable and actionable things, we must make this data smaller and easier to understand. How do we go about this? By converting the input rows into fewer rows or a single number.

For example, from 10,000 rows of customer purchase data, you can calculate the total sales, average sales, sales by month, and sales by product.

This is the **output**. We also refer to it as Reports, Dashboards, Aggregations or Summary.

Take in a large amount of information and compress it into a compact summary.

Now, let's go and look at what exactly we mean by "clean data." You will be surprised to know that there is no simple and standard way to check whether your data is clean.

This isn't a problem, however. Here is a simple 11-item checklist to help you.

Clean data checklist

Data can be text, numbers, dates, and so on. Just entering or importing the data into Excel (or any other spreadsheet) is not enough. The data must be *CLEAN*. Unfortunately, hitherto, there has not been any simple definition of what *clean* means. Here is a simple 11-item checklist.

If your data passes each item, then it is clean. Here is the checklist:

Check for every column		
	Each column must have a heading (not data).	Headings cannot have data. For example, Jan and Feb are NOT headings.
	No blank headings.	Columns without names are confusing.
	No duplicate headings.	Duplicate headings are confusing and can lead to errors while interpreting data.
	No formulas in headings.	Why? We will see later (in the **Tables** section)
	No merged cells.	This is INPUT data. Why do we need merged cells in the input data? Output – or a report – may require merged cells. That is fine.
	No grand or subtotals.	The same as the previous point.
	No formatting instead of data.	Why? You cannot analyze formatting. For example, you cannot get the total number of yellow cells.
	One column, one meaning.	This is a frequent problem. More columns means better analysis.

Check for whole data		
	One column, one data type.	Check by looking at alignment. Crucial for dates.
Data grows vertically (not horizontally).		It is more efficient to add more data below existing data.
	Related data must be in a single sheet (or data model)	Once the data is clean, as per the 10 rules previously, it is still going to grow. It should grow vertically. That means, if you get multiple pieces of clean, related data, then you should keep it in ONE block, and not in separate sheets or files. Example: The same type of data arriving each month, or from different regions. Why? Because you cannot analyze sheet names or files. You can only analyze data that is in a column.

It is important to understand this concept. Watch this video to see examples of each item. The video shows each rule with sample data and explains why it is important to follow the rule. It shows the wrong format first. It explains why it is wrong and then shows the correct format.

hi.switchy.io/excd

You should compare these examples with your own data and learn how to apply these rules.

How to use this checklist

Look at your data – each column as well as overall. Check which items are not right and then clean them up or repair them. We will cover common clean-up scenarios in the next section. Finally, once the data is clean, convert it to a table.

How to capture clean data

Often, data is already there. You export it from business applications or people send it to you as files. But what if you want to capture data from scratch?

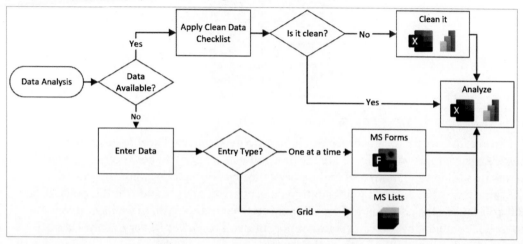

Figure 4.2 – The data management process

Entry types can be a form or a grid. Let's understand the difference between them.

We have two apps available: Microsoft Forms and Microsoft Lists. Forms is ideal for conducting surveys or polls. Here we have a page with multiple questions. One person usually fills only ONE form.

If you need to capture business data, a grid is better, with rows and columns of data. One person enters multiple rows and columns at a time. Traditionally, everyone uses Excel for such data entry. However, using Microsoft Lists is a much better choice because it always gives clean data.

Therefore, let's learn how to capture fresh data using Microsoft Lists.

Entering clean data using Lists

We often need to get data from multiple persons. The most frequent method used for this is to send an Excel file to each person. Excel is not the ideal way to capture raw or input data. Trust me, Microsoft Lists is much better for capturing clean data effortlessly.

Don't believe me? Then download this `detailed PDF`.

`https://hi.switchy.io/4m6C`

Microsoft Lists works on any browser. There is no need to have Excel or any other app. Decide the columns you want. Share the link and you are good to go. You can prevent errors by adding validations and mandatory columns. Multiple persons can enter data at the same time or at different points in time. Each person can see and edit their own data. But you can see the entire data. There is no need to copy and paste as we have automatic consolidation. Finally, you can create a report in Excel or Power BI very easily. Data increased? No problem. Just refresh the report.

Now you know why Lists is the way to go. Let's see how to use it. Where do you find Microsoft Lists? In **Office 365 | All apps**.

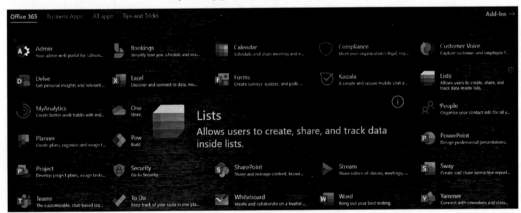

Figure 4.3 – Start using Microsoft Lists

This is the process for entering data using Microsoft Lists. Simple, secure, fast, and efficient.

Create List   Add Columns   Share Link   Enter Data   Analyze Data

Figure 4.4 – How to use Lists

Watch this video for a detailed demo of how to create a list, capture data, and create reports. Multiple persons can add data securely without interfering with each other's data. You can then connect Excel to the Lists data and create reports. This is a 2-hour session recording.

hi.switchy.io/mslst

Creating a new list

Start with a blank list. A new list always has one text type of column called **Title**. Rename it to another text column that you need. This is a mandatory column.

Adding columns

Adding new columns is easy. Click on the **Add Column** button and choose the type of column. These are more powerful than what you get with Excel. Explore all types of columns before you decide what you need.

Once you choose the type of column, look at the options as well. One of the options is to make the column entry mandatory. That means, if this column is blank, you cannot save the entire row.

Sharing with people

Now, click the **Share** button and add the email IDs of people who will enter data into this list. You are the owner – therefore, you can add, update, and remove everything.

Setting security

When other parties are adding data, you do not want them to see each other's data.

To provide this type of security, click on the wheel in the top-right corner – **List Settings**. Choose **Advanced Settings**, and then make sure people can *read and edit their own data*.

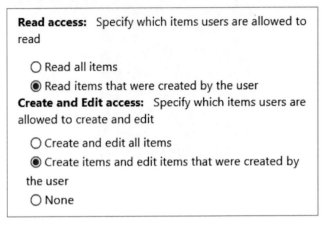

Figure 4.5 – Secure data entry with Lists

Data entry

The recipients will receive a link in an email. They can just open the link in the browser and start editing data. For adding data – one row at a time – use the + **New** button. To add multiple rows, like in Excel, choose **Edit in grid view**.

Figure 4.6 – Data entry methods

Multiple persons can add data at the same time. People outside your organization will need to receive and add an **OTP** (short for **one-time password**) to begin data entry.

Creating views

You can see all the data at any time. You can sort, filter, group the data, and even apply conditional formatting. You can create multiple views for quick access. Explore views and understand which one to use for your data. Make sure that you try the **Calendar** view with the date type of columns.

Connecting to Excel

If you want to summarize and analyze the data further, choose **Export to Excel**. You will expect an Excel file to download. But it does not – you get something better – an IQY file. Do not worry. Just double-click the file; it will still open in Excel. But it will keep the connection with our list. You will get all the data in a sheet as an Excel table. You can add more calculated columns as needed.

Make sure to refresh this data every time you open the Excel file. Click inside the data and choose the **Table Design** tab | **Refresh** drop-down | **Connection Properties...** | **Refresh data when opening the file**.

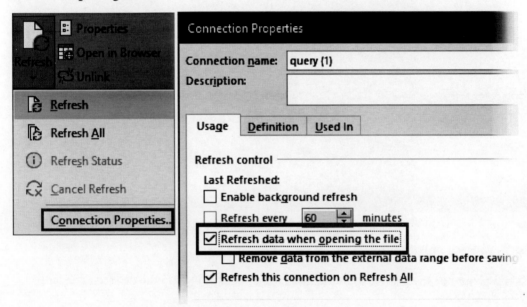

Figure 4.7 – Auto-refresh

Creating reports from Lists data

If you want to summarize or analyze the data, you can now use PivotTables or Power BI.

Data captured using Lists is usually clean, as per our checklist, because Lists follows all these rules anyway.

Next, we will see how to get data into Excel by just capturing a photo, without manual data entry.

Automatic data entry from photos

The Excel mobile app (or the Office mobile app) has an extremely useful feature: automatic data entry. Just take a photo of any printed table and convert it into an Excel sheet. This can make manual data entry obsolete and increase accuracy as well.

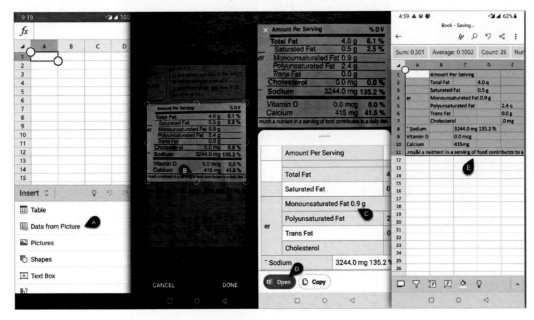

Figure 4.8 – Automatic data entry from pictures

Open an Excel file and choose **Insert | Data from Picture**.

Take a picture of any printed item that has tabular data in it, crop the desired area, and then click **Done**.

Now, Excel will use AI to recognize the text and convert it to data. This is currently in preview mode. You can change data or correct any mistakes.

Now choose **Open**. The Excel sheet opens with the data. Cool stuff!

Importing and cleaning up using Power Query

Power Query enables amazingly fast data cleanup – no manual work, no complex formulas, no macros, no programming. Introducing "Power Query" – your complete data cleanup toolkit!

If you have older versions of Excel, you can download and install the **Power Query** add-in: `https://www.microsoft.com/en-in/download/details.aspx?id=39379`. This will add a separate Power Query tab. In both cases, the features are similar.

With Excel 2016 upward, Power Query is available in the **Data** tab | **Get & Transform Data**. This replaces the old **Get External Data** option.

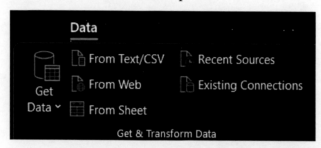

Figure 4.9 – Get & Transform Data

You can import from 40+ data sources – flat files, databases, PDFs, web pages, and more. Once you specify the source, the powerful cleanup tool – Power Query – opens.

There are numerous data cleanup requirements. We cannot cover all of them here. However, you can see this video playlist for details: `https://hi.switchy.io/fyidc`.

> **Try to Use Power Query for All Existing Data Cleanup Tasks**
>
> This is important. Even if your current method is working, whether it is a manual process or a macro, try Power Query. You will be surprised to know its power and flexibility. This is the only way in which Power Query can add value instantly.

Let's explore Power Query with three common scenarios of bad data – crosstab, unwanted gaps in data, and multiple CSV consolidation.

Power Query is also available in Power BI Desktop. Choose the **Home** tab | **Get Data** and choose the data source. Click the **Transform** button while importing the data to invoke Power Query.

Crosstab data

Often, data has two mixed tables – one horizontal and one vertical. This is known as a crosstab. In the following example, the horizontal table has product names, and the vertical table has months. Use the following sample file: `Ch4 – Excel – Cross Tab Unpivot.xlsx`.

		Vertical Table				
	Product	Jan	Feb	Mar	Apr	May
Horizontal Table	Mask	101	199	191	96	26
	Sanitizer	191	70	51	171	160
	Gloves	24	14	193	127	77
	Tissue	172	12	110	108	143

Figure 4.10 – Crosstab data

If you apply our clean data checklist, you will realize that each column does *not* have a heading. Jan, Feb, and so on are not headings – they are data. That is why this type of data is difficult to analyze. Combining multiple pieces of crosstab data – across multiple years, in this case – is time-consuming and error-prone.

This data looks like a PivotTable output, but it is not a pivot. It is just raw data.

Ideally, we just need three columns: **Product**, **Month**, and **Amount**.

But we do not want to do this cleanup manually. That will require row-by-row copying and pasting and repeated special transposition. That is where Power Query comes in.

Download this file and try it out: `Ch4 – Excel – Cross Tab Unpivot.xlsx>`.Let's get started:

1. Select the **Data** tab and choose **Get and Transform | From Sheet** (or **From Table/ Range**) . This converts the range to a table. Make sure that you include the headers in the table. Then, click **OK**.

Figure 4.11 – Importing data from sheet

2. Now, a separate window opens – this is the Power Query window. Explore Power Query and get familiar with it. Power Query is a common method of cleaning up data from all available data sources.

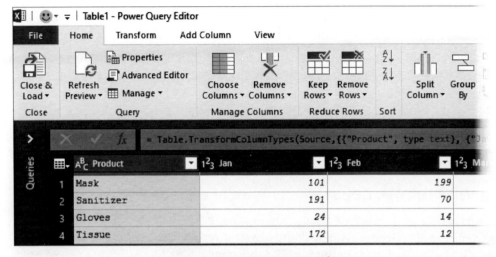

Figure 4.12 – Power Query window

Initially, it just shows the original data. Now it is up to you to decide how to clean it up. We want bulk transposition of the month columns.

3. Right-click on the "good" column, which is the **Product** column in our case, and choose **Unpivot Other Columns**.

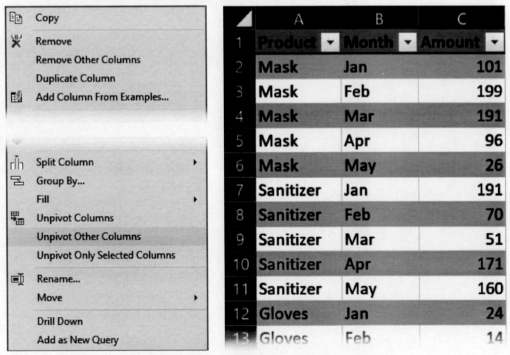

Figure 4.13 – Unpivot Other Columns option and results

4. Now you have two columns as expected. Double-click the column heading and rename the **Attribute** and **Value** columns to **Month** and **Amount**.

5. Click the **Home | Close and Load** option to get the clean data. It will appear on a new sheet (see the left screen in *Figure 4.13*). Remember, Power Query never changes the original data.

6. Later, if the original (input) data changes, right-click in the output and choose **Refresh**. Power Query remembers the steps you took to clean the data. Refreshing just repeats the steps. This is how you save an enormous amount of time.

Data with blank cells

Here we have data with unwanted blank cells. This happens when you copy and paste values from a pivot table or when you dump a system report. Use the Ch4 - Excel - Blank Cells.xlsx file to try this out. Use this sample file Ch4 - Excel - Blank Cells.xlsx.

	A	B	C
4	**Year**	**Month**	**Amount**
5	FY 19	Jan	33
6			38
7			56
8		Feb	68
9			72
10			88
11	FY 20	Jan	86
12			42
13			86
14		Feb	72
15			98
16			71
17			55
18			29

Figure 4.14 – Fill unwanted gaps instantly

This is easy. Select the data – **Data** tab | **From Sheet** and then click **OK** to add a table with headers. Now, the Power Query window will open. Select the columns that have empty cells and right-click – **Fill** | **Down**. Done!

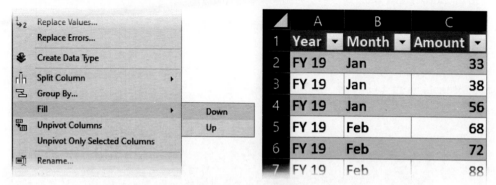

Figure 4.15 – Fill | Down option

Data in multiple CSV files

The consolidation of multiple CSV files is a common requirement. Each CSV should have the same columns and data types. There is no need to manually open and copy and paste data from each file. Power Query can do this in a few clicks.

Go to **Data** | **Get External Data** | **Get data** | **File** | **Folder**. Choose the folder containing the CSV files. Power Query will show a list of the files and ask you what action you want to take. Choose **Combine and Load**.

Power Query needs to use one of the files as the sample file to find out the structure of the data. By default, it uses the first file. Click **OK** to allow the first file as a sample file.

Now, Power Query does all the necessary work to give you combined data. And next month, when more files land in the folder? No problem. Just go to the output, right-click, and refresh!

Watch this video for more details: `https://youtu.be/-ChtiKoohjc`.

In short, Power Query automates the cleanup process and increases accuracy. We have only scratched the surface of what Power Query can do. Learn more about data cleanup by using this YouTube playlist: `https://hi.switchy.io/fyidc`.

Now that we have clean data, the next step is to keep it clean and make it easy to access. Once the input data is clean, we must convert it to Excel tables. Let's now see why Excel tables are so important when it comes to efficient and smart data management.

Importance of Excel tables

Once the data is clean, we must convert it to a table. Excel tables are the best way to manage input data in Excel.

Select the data and go to the **Insert** tab and then click **Table**. Excel tries to detect whether the data has a header. Click **OK**. The data is now a table.

You will see the **Table Design** tab appear when you click inside any table. Always change the default table name to a recognizable name.

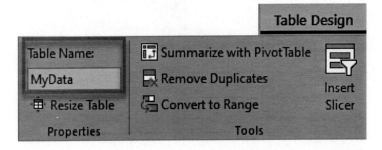

Figure 4.16 – Specifying a table name

Two practical uses of table names are as follows:

- The name is usable in formulas – making it easy to understand (self-documenting). For example, if you want the total amount from a table named My data, you can write this formula in any sheet:

  = *sum(Mydata [Amount])*

- The second benefit is instant navigation. If you want to go to a particular table, there is no need to search. Go to the **Name** box, open the dropdown, and select the table name – instant navigation.

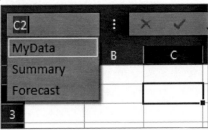

Figure 4.17 – Instant navigation

Why am I insisting on keeping the data as a table? Some people think adding tables increases the file size. It does not. And, more importantly, a table provides many benefits:

- Automatic updating of dependent formulas, charts, and pivots (requires manual refresh)

- Automatic formula copying in calculated columns

- More readable structured formulas (for example, `[@Amount] - [@Tax]` instead of `b3-c3`)

- Automatic headers – no need to freeze the pane

- Automatic formatting and validation copying

- Delete rows/columns without affecting outside data

- Automatic totals

- Accurate import for Power Query/Power BI

- Instant navigation

- Dynamic array formulas

There are many more advantages apart from these.

You can watch this video to learn all the benefits of tables in 10 minutes:

https://hi.switchy.io/34hk

The most important one is that tables update all dependents – formulas, charts, pivot ranges – that are based on the table data automatically. You save lots of time and minimize errors (operational risk).

> **Tip**
> All clean raw data must be in tables.

Now that we have clean **input** data, we can start analyzing it. To recap, all raw data must be in Excel tables. This simplifies further analysis and manipulation.

Data analysis

Input data is usually long. There are hundreds (or thousands) of rows and dozens of columns. Just scrolling or filtering input data does not help us understand what is happening. We need to summarize the data first – convert thousands of rows into a few rows and columns (or values) with totals, averages, and ratios. We do so by following these steps:

1. Use the **Analyze Data** option in Excel.
2. Create reports using **PivotTables** and **PivotChart**.
3. Create interactive reports using **Power BI**.

Before we learn all this, what if your data is already small and summarized? In this case, just use **Quick Analysis** in Excel. It is a powerful way to understand data instantly.

Quick Analysis

If the data is small enough, we can analyze it easily. Remember that we want to learn all possible useful things from the data. Excel gives us a powerful way of looking at the same data from different points of view – with minimal effort. This is Quick Analysis. Just select the data and choose **Quick Analysis** from the SmartTag icon that appears (or from the right-click menu). You can use the following sample file to try this out and learn: `Ch4 - Excel - numbers.xlsx`.

Product	Apr	May
Mask	57	67
Gloves	100	83
Sanitizer	90	57
Tissue	62	34
Vaccine	50	55

Quick Analysis (Ctrl+Q)

Use the Quick Analysis tool to quickly and easily analyze your data with some of Excel's most useful tools, such as charts, color-coding, and formulas.

Figure 4.18 – Quick Analysis

Click on the icon to see 25 ways to visualize and interpret the data. Choose each category, move the mouse cursor over each option, and see how the data changes. Five types of analysis are available – **Formatting**, **Charts**, **Totals**, **Tables**, and **Sparklines** (mini charts).

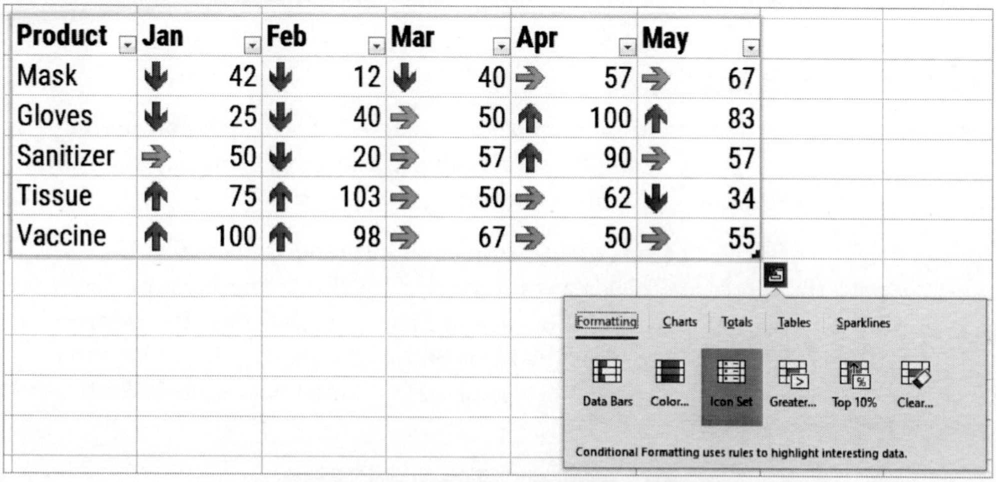

Product	Jan	Feb	Mar	Apr	May
Mask	42	12	40	57	67
Gloves	25	40	50	100	83
Sanitizer	50	20	57	90	57
Tissue	75	103	50	62	34
Vaccine	100	98	67	50	55

Figure 4.19 – Icon sets – low, medium, and high values

Here is the same data using another form of visualization – mini-charts called Sparklines.

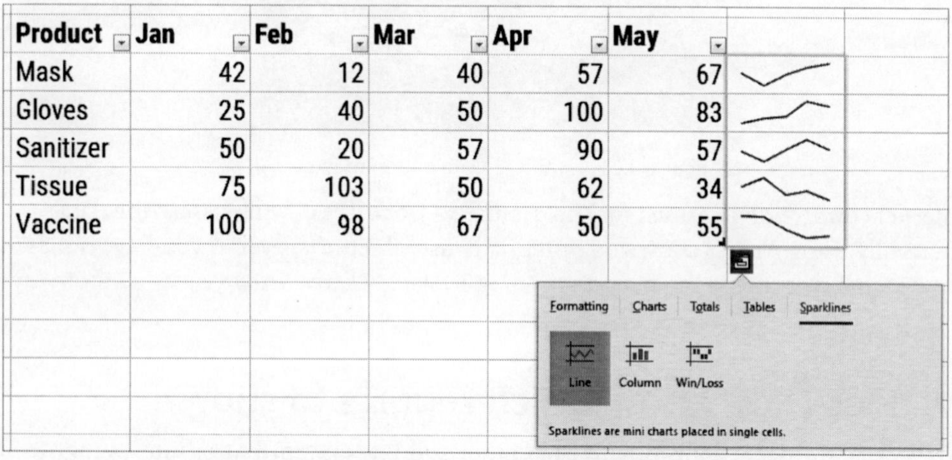

Product	Jan	Feb	Mar	Apr	May
Mask	42	12	40	57	67
Gloves	25	40	50	100	83
Sanitizer	50	20	57	90	57
Tissue	75	103	50	62	34
Vaccine	100	98	67	50	55

Figure 4.20 – Sparklines – see fluctuation across rows

Here you can see a separate mini chart for each line of data. These charts are known as sparklines. The chart fits into a single cell and shows the fluctuations clearly. This is the best way to compare the pattern across rows of data – without overlap.

Each different visual will help you understand various aspects of the same data and help you learn all the necessary useful things quickly. Once you learn something, you can decide how to act on it and improve your work in the future.

Make sure you see all the Quick Analysis options for every piece of summary data you have. When the data changes, see the options again.

Now, let's see how AI can help us analyze data in a smart way.

Analyzing data using AI

We saw how to get quick reports. But remember, we want to derive all possible useful information from the data. How many questions will you ask? How many reports will you create? That sounds like a time-consuming and ambiguous process.

Fortunately, you do not have to waste time creating multiple reports manually. There is a simple but powerful way to analyze data without selecting visuals and fields manually. It uses AI to answer your questions. Click inside the data and then choose the **Home** tab | the **Analyze Data** button (known as the **Ideas** button previously). Please note that this feature is available in the Microsoft 365 version of Excel (and not in the desktop versions such as 2016 or 2019).

Figure 4.21 – Analyze Data button in Excel

An internet connection is a must for this feature to work. Excel will analyze the data automatically using AI and show you potentially useful reports, even if you have not asked for any specific report. Use the file : Ch4 Excel Data for analysis.xlsx to try this out

How does Excel know which reports to show?

It correlates all the data columns with each other and finds important or interesting information (statistically significant) using AI.

You must at least look at all the Analyze Data reports one by one. Whichever report looks interesting or useful, click the **Insert** button. Now, Excel will add a new sheet and the PivotTable and/or chart. You can then explore it in detail and apply your business knowledge to decide the plan of action.

Remember to do this with every input data you have. Even if the data is familiar, you may find more useful and actionable information. Less effort – more impact.

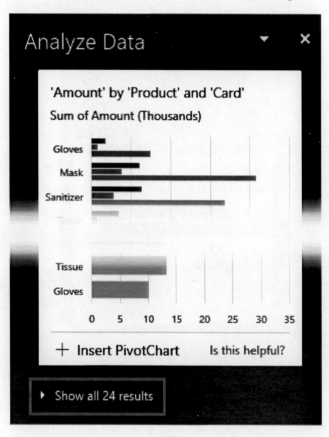

Figure 4.22 – Look at all the Analyze Data reports

Asking Excel a question

In addition to showing important reports, Analyze Data also helps you to explore the data using simple English language questions. Type your question in the textbox and Excel will give you the answer in the form of a PivotTable or chart automatically. No need to type formulas!

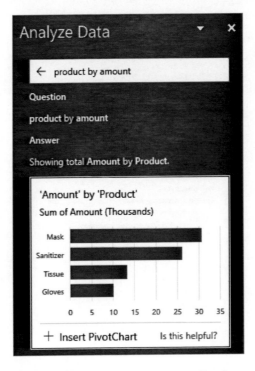

Figure 4.23 – Putting questions to Excel

If you want to analyze it further, choose the **Insert PivotChart** (or **Insert PivotTable**) option.

Excel uses AI to answer these questions. You can ask complicated questions such as the following:

- Which are the top three dates by amount?
- How many cities are there?
- Which is the city with the largest average amount?
- What is the amount per product, excluding gloves?
- What is the total amount per product and card?

This is the fastest way of getting the analysis you want. This can save you an enormous amount of time. We will explore pivot tables and charts in the upcoming sections.

Creating reports with PivotTables

You can add all these AI-based reports as pivot tables. If you want to create a report exactly the way you want, create a pivot table directly.

Make sure that the data is clean, convert it to a table, click inside it, and choose **Insert | PivotTable**. You should see four options – we will go with the first one (**From Table/Range**).

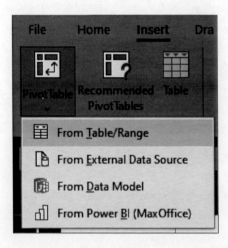

Figure 4.24 – Insert PivotTable from table/range

Excel will add a new sheet and a new blank report. On the right side, you can see **PivotTable Fields**, which is the list of columns in the input data table. Below the list, you get four places to drag and drop columns: **Rows**, **Columns**, **Values**, and **Filters**. Remember that calculations can only happen in the **Values** area.

Let's use the same input data and create a report showing **Country** in **Rows, Product** in **Columns,** and **Sum of Amount** in **Values.** Just drag each field to the correct area and create the report you want; instant reports without adding any manual formulas.

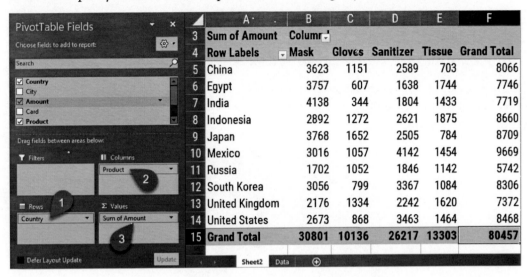

Figure 4.25 – Pivot table – Rows, Columns, Values

Try different things with the data and learn how to use pivot tables. When you add more to the input table, right-click inside the pivot table and select **Refresh.** The pivot table will now show the latest report.

Show Values As

To summarize a numeric column, drag it to the **Values** area. By default, **Sum** aggregation will be used. If the column has one or more text or blank values, then the default calculation becomes **Count.** You can always change it using the **Summarize By** option.

Want to see the subtotals as percentages? No problem. Right-click in the **Values** column, choose **Show Values As,** and choose **% of Column Total** as in the following screenshot. You can add the same column twice in the **Values** area so that you can see the actual values as well as the percentages.

Row Labels ⯆	Sum of Amount	Sum of Amount2	
Beijing	8066	10.03%	No Calculation
Cairo	7746	9.63%	% of Grand Total
Jakarta	8660	10.76%	✓ % of Column Total
London	7372	9.16%	% of Row Total
Mexico City	9669	12.02%	% Of...
Moscow	5742	7.14%	% of Parent Row Total
New Delhi	7719	9.59%	% of Parent Column Total
Seoul	8306	10.32%	% of Parent Total...
Tokyo	8709	10.82%	Difference From...
Washington	8468	10.52%	% Difference From...
Grand Total	**80457**	**100.00%**	Running Total In...
			% Running Total In...
			Rank Smallest to Largest...
			Rank Largest to Smallest...
			Index

Figure 4.26 – Totals and percentages using Show Values As

This may look like a long and confusing list, but you must learn all of these. However, it is quite simple, really. Try them out with the sample data first and then your own data. You can circumvent hours of manual work using these options.

Watch this 25-minute video to learn how to use **Show Values As** in detail:

hi.switchy.io/exsva

Charts and PivotCharts

Once a pivot table is ready, you can see the same data as charts. Of course, you can create charts directly from the input data, but it is easier and better to do it with summarized data in a pivot table. The same chart types are available in both cases.

Click inside a pivot table, open the **PivotTable Analyze** tab, and select **PivotChart**. Select the type of chart you want. When you change the PivotTable, the **PivotChart** changes automatically. You can filter data using the dropdowns showing field names.

Do not worry about these extra buttons. When you copy and paste a **PivotChart** to PowerPoint, these buttons disappear automatically.

Creating interactive reports using Power BI

Power BI is another tool available in Microsoft 365. It comes in two flavors – one is the desktop version, which is completely free, and the server version, which you do not need on day one.

Although it is free, Power BI Desktop is extremely powerful, yet extremely easy to use.

Figure 4.27 – Power BI Desktop

Go to the Microsoft Store in Windows 10 and install Power BI Desktop. Log in using your Microsoft 365 account.

You already know how to import data in Excel using **Get & Transform data** (Power Query). The good news is that Power BI uses the same system to import and clean up data. That means you already know half of Power BI. Now let's see how this is done:

1. Download the Ch4 Excel Data for analysis.xlsx file in a folder. Do not open it in Excel.

2.   Go to **Power BI Desktop | Get data | Excel**.

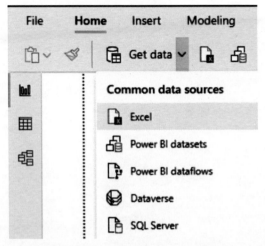

Figure 4.28 – Importing from Excel

3.   Choose the file from the folder. The file will open and show sheets as well as tables. Choose the **mydata** table.

4.   Choose the **Load** option. Transform means cleanup. We do not require cleanup here because the data is already clean.

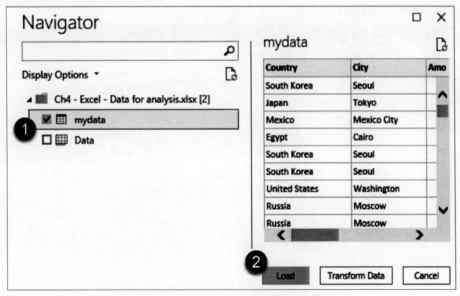

Figure 4.29 – Loading a table from Excel

Power BI has three areas: **Report**, **Data**, and **Model**. We already have our table in the **Data** area. Check it out.

5. Now let's make an interactive report. Keep saving the Power BI file periodically. It uses the PBIX extension.

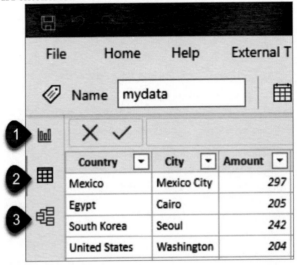

Figure 4.30 – Power BI: 1 – Report, 2 – Data, 3 – Model

6. Go to the **Reports** tab (1 in Figure 4.31). It looks different, but at heart, it is still drag and drop, like pivot tables. Make sure you keep the **Visualizations** (2) and **Fields** (3) areas open and close the **Filters** area.

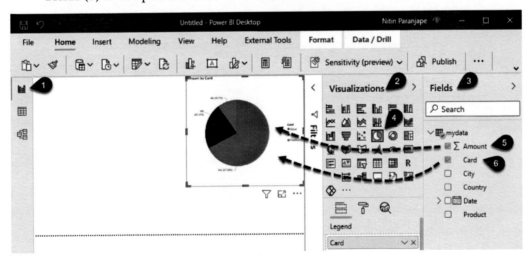

Figure 4.31 – How to create charts in Power BI

Explore all the available visuals – just look at each tooltip.

7. Now, click on the **Pie chart** visual (4). An empty pie chart appears. Now, drag and drop **Amount** and **Card** on top of the pie chart (5 and 6). Now the pie chart is ready.

8. In the same way, create two more visuals – a **Column** chart with **Amount** and **Product**, and one more, a line chart with **Month** on the *x* axis and **Amount** on the *y* axis.

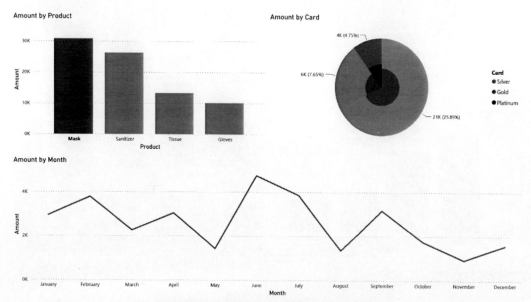

Figure 4.32 – Power BI report with filter on Mask

Your report will look like this. Now, click on one column, for example, **Mask**, and see what happens.

It filters all other visuals. This way, you get an **interactive report** instantly without programming. Technically, this is known as cross-filtering.

You can use this sample file: `Ch4 - Power BI - Sample.pbix`. It has multiple pages at the bottom. The first page, **Interactive Report**, shows the example below.

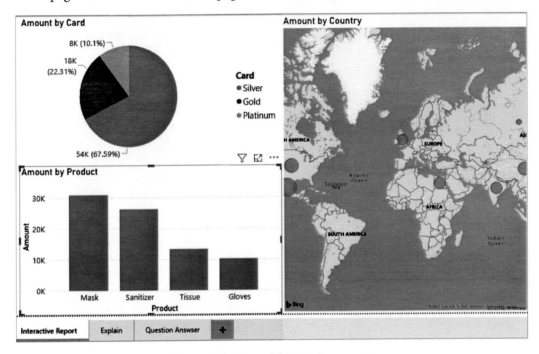

Figure 4.33 – Power BI interactive report

Explore Power BI and use it. Do not wait for anyone to request Power BI reports. You already have the data in Excel, CSV, or elsewhere. Just import the same data and analyze it in Power BI. It will help you immensely.

Like Excel, Power BI can also answer your questions about the data. It is more powerful compared to Excel. Just double-click on an empty area of the report page and **Q&A** appears. Ask queries and get answers instantly. Show this off to your colleagues and bosses.

Before we go, let's learn an extremely powerful feature. Go to the **Explain** page in the sample report file. It shows the amount for each month. There was a big decrease from July to August, and anyone will ask the question – why?

But can you answer it instantly? No. We do not have that explanation report ready. Most people will say, "I will get back to you." Right?

Wrong! You can explain it instantly. Right-click on the July point and choose **Analyze | Explain the decrease**.

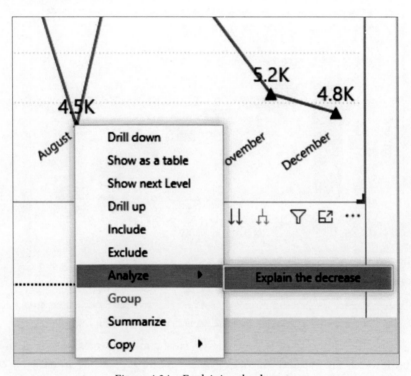

Figure 4.34 – Explaining the decrease

And miraculously, Power BI analyzes all your data to show the reasons for that decrease. Scroll down to see each influencing factor (column) as a separate chart.

The first column shows the amount for July, while the last column shows the amount for August. In between is the breakdown of what caused the decrease. Is this not amazing?

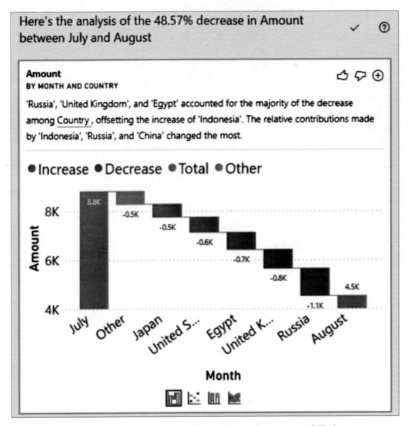

Figure 4.35 – Decrease in value explained as a waterfall chart

This is just a very quick glimpse of Power BI. I am sure you want to explore it further. As a starting point, watch the popular video, *Power BI walkthrough for beginners*. It is an old video (2015), but the concepts are still the same. The menus may look a little different, but all options are still available: https://youtu.be/h6AIAxMEDiw.

Remember the definition of analytics we covered at the beginning of this chapter? Does it make sense now? Do you realize how easy it is to learn all possible useful things and manage your business better than ever before?

So far, we have only looked at the analytical tools available in Excel and Power BI. All along, you may be wondering as to when we are going to learn Excel functions. Well, it is now time to learn "how to learn" Excel functions. Let's dive straight into it.

Which Excel functions to learn and how

We have only covered the analytics part of Excel. But what about the 650+ Excel functions? Before you say, "Oh, I do not need so many," just relax. You do not need to learn all the functions. However, it should not be the case that you need a function but do not know that it exists. That is inefficiency!

The only way to know the functions you need is to just look at all of them once and shortlist the ones that are useful to you. Just spend 20 minutes doing this exercise.

Step	Activity	Time
1	Shortlist potentially useful functions.	Maximum of 20 minutes – once per lifetime!
2	Learn these functions one by one.	1 to 30 minutes per function, depending upon the complexity
3	Use these functions in relevant places with new as well as existing Excel files.	Ongoing

Shortlisting useful functions

Now let's explore and find the functions which appear to be useful and relevant for your work:

1. Open a Word document (or better still, a OneNote page). You will add the names of useful functions to it.

2. Add a table with two columns – **Function Name** and **Where can I use it**. Go to the **Formulas** menu and choose **Insert Function**. You will see a list of the most recently used functions. Let's ignore those for now.

3. Open the **Select a category** dropdown. Skip the **All** category. Go to the next one, for example, **Financial**. If you are not from the finance field, you will still need these functions for managing personal finance. We will use the **Finance** category as an example. You must repeat this process for each category.

You can skip categories that are completely irrelevant to your work. For example, if you are a medical doctor, you can skip the **Math** and **Trig** functions.

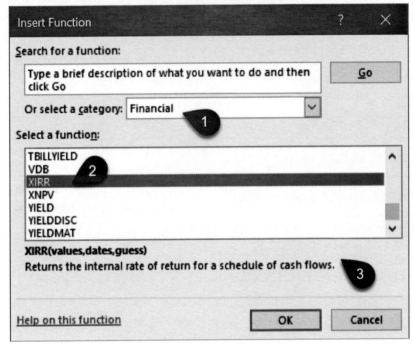

Figure 4.36 – Learning Excel functions

4. Click on the first function listed. The first financial function will be **ACCRINT**. Below the list, you will see a one-line description of what this function does. Read it. If you are already familiar with it, skip it.

    If you think the function is relevant and useful (for example, **XIRR**), just add it to your notes. Do not try to learn the function right away. We are just making a list right now. Make sure to add the scenario where you want to use the function in the second column.

5. Press the down arrow to move to the next function, read the description, and skip or shortlist it. Repeat this process for all functions.

6. Move to the next category and repeat the process. It will not take more than a few minutes for you. This is time very well spent.

At the end of this exercise, you will have a list of functions that you need to learn. So let's learn how to learn!

How to learn any Excel function

We must learn all the shortlisted functions one by one. Take your time, but set a deadline and stick to it. How do you learn functions? Simple. Go to the same **Insert Function** dialog, find the function, and click the **Help** option on this function link.

This will open the detailed help text in a separate window on the right side or a separate web page. Read the help text from top to bottom. Try to understand the inputs, the optional parameters, the logic, and the output. Scroll down to the **Examples** section. Every function on the Excel help page has one or more examples, with data, formula(s), and output.

If the application of the function is simple enough to understand just by looking at the help text and examples, that is great! Move on to the next function.

For complex functions or for those that have multiple parameters and variations, you cannot learn it just by reading the examples. The best way is to try it out yourself, play with it, change the data and parameters, and figure it out.

Here is the exact process for practicing any function:

Create a new Excel file and save it with a sensible name (for example, ExcelLearn. xlsx). Use this file to try out all the newly learned functions. This will be a useful reference for you in the future. Follow these steps:

1. Add a new sheet to the ExcelLearn file. Make sure you are at the A1 cell.

2. Open the Help menu for the function you want to learn.

3. Scroll to the **Examples** section on the Help page.

4. Select the entire example – with data, formulas, and output.

5. Copy it (*Ctrl + C*).

6. Paste it at *A1* in the new sheet.

7. Click on the clipboard icon and choose the second option – **Match Destination Formatting (M)**. Resize the columns so that you can see things clearly.

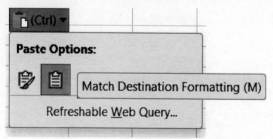

Figure 4.37 – Paste with destination formatting

8. Click the cell that has the formula and press *F2* to edit it.

9. Learn the formula and try different variations.

Finally, when you have finished doing all this, it is time to use it in your day-to-day work.

Applying these functions to your files

There are two elements here: new files and existing files.

Using these functions in a new file is easy. You know the function and the scenario where you need it. Just do it.

For existing files, it can be a more laborious process. While learning the new functions, you may have noticed that you have been using other, less efficient functions or complex formulas. Now, you need to go back to your existing files and replace those with new functions.

It is always safer to create a new copy/version of existing files before you replace existing functions.

Finally, if you have found a new, useful function, there is a good chance that your colleagues/organization may also find it useful. Share this knowledge with others.

Next, let's look at a common need – conducting surveys and polls. People use Word or Excel for this or use third-party tools such as SurveyMonkey or Google Forms. But you may not have explored the Forms app, which is a part of Microsoft 365. Let's explore Forms.

Surveys and polls

You can conduct polls, surveys, and quizzes using Microsoft Forms. It is a part of Microsoft 365. You can find it under **All apps**. This is also data entry. But here, we enter one row at a time. And usually, one person completes just one form, which means one row.

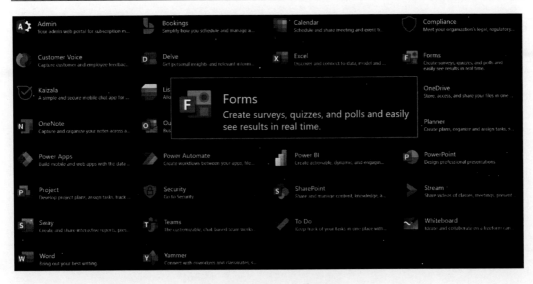

Figure 4.38 – Microsoft Forms

Creating a survey

The process is simple. Like Lists, it is a five-step process.

Create Form   Add Questions   Share Link   Enter Data   Analyze Data

Figure 4.39 – Conducting polls using Forms

Surveys

A survey is an online form. You can complete it on any browser, including on cell phones. There is no special app for it. Creation, data entry, and analysis – they all happen on a browser.

Create a survey and specify the title, description, base image, and theme. Use the **Preview** option while you are designing the form. Preview on mobile as well as desktop. Forms adjust automatically to any screen size.

Settings

Before adding questions, go to **Settings** and choose the right options. It is good to manage settings at this stage because later, you tend to forget.

Decide who can respond to the survey: internal staff or external people such as customers, dealers, and suppliers.

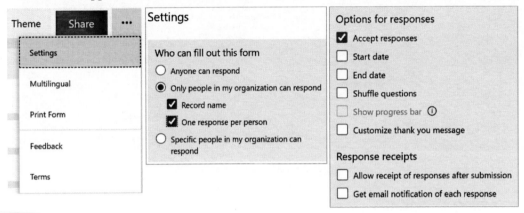

Figure 4.40 – Share and Settings options for form

Internal staff must log in to complete the survey. Here you can accept one response per person. Outside people just click on the link and fill in the form without logging in. Therefore, we cannot restrict it to one response per person.

Now let's add the questions.

Adding questions

Eight types of questions are available (as of June 2021): **Rating**, **Text**, **Date**, **Choice**, **Ranking**, **Likert**, **Net Promoter Score**, and **File Upload**. Create a test survey with each type of question. Add three to four entries and look at the **Responses** tab. That will help you understand what type of analysis you get for each type of question.

Here is an example of how the **Rating** question appears and how its analysis appears.

Figure 4.41 – Survey analysis of the Rating score

Sharing the form

Create the survey, preview it, and then click the **Share** button.

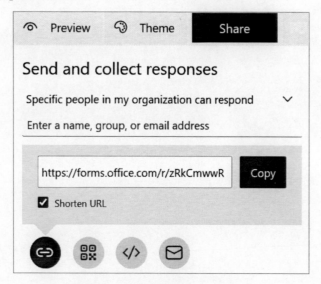

Figure 4.42 – Survey sharing options

Choose the type – org or external – and choose the method of sharing – simple hyperlink, QR code, embed code, or email. Embed code is useful for adding this link to another web page.

Analysis

A survey will remain open for anywhere between a few hours and a few weeks, depending upon the goals. In any case, you can see a live analysis of the survey data at any time. Click on the **Responses** tab to see the analysis for each question. Click the **Insights** button, if available, to see more details.

Finally, you can export the data to Excel for further analysis. Once in Excel, we can use pivot tables and/or Power BI to analyze the data in greater detail.

The Forms app is also able to create online evaluations. Let's see how we can create instant quizzes using Forms.

Quizzes

The process is the same as for surveys. The only difference is that for quizzes, each question has a score. If the question is of the multiple-choice type, the scoring is automatic.

Creating quiz questions

Create the question, specifying the options along with the correct choice, hints, and score.

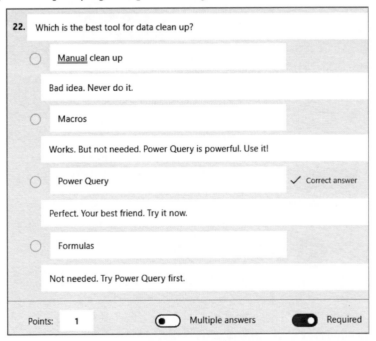

Figure 4.43 – Multiple-choice question

Scoring the quiz

For multiple-choice questions, scoring is automatic. If a question type does not support automatic scoring, you can enter the manual score for each question of each candidate. You can also check individual candidate responses using the **Review answers** option.

Figure 4.44 – Reviewing quiz answers

Once the scoring is complete, choose **Post scores**. Here you can see the results for each candidate.

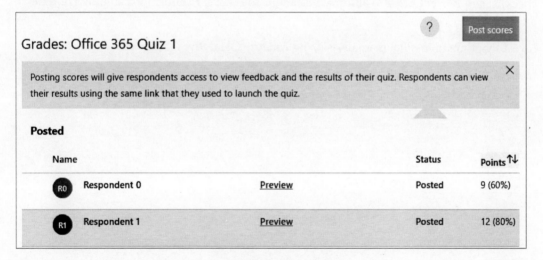

Figure 4.45 – Quiz results

If it was an internal quiz (with login), then each candidate can click on the original quiz link and see their own results.

Automation after submission

Finally, using Power Automate, you can take automatic action as soon as someone submits the form. For example, if a customer gives a poor rating, you want to send an apology mail instantly and automatically. We will learn Power Automate in *Chapter 8, Automating Work without Programming*.

Inserting a quiz in training videos

Videos are a common way to teach staff members. For storing videos, Stream is the best place (*Chapter 5, Managing Files Efficiently*). After someone watches a video, why not give them a quiz too? We will see how to do this in the *Stream* section in *Chapter 5, Managing Files Efficiently*.

Summary

That brings us to the beginning of your data journey. Right – the beginning – not the end!

This was just a whirlwind tour of the various components. Now it is your job to apply this learning to your data, repair or revamp the data capture processes, and use the clean data checklist and Power Query to automate cleanup. You will save enormous amounts of time by doing this.

Invest that time in intelligent analysis using Analyze Data, PivotTables, and Power BI.

In the next chapter, we will see how to manage files efficiently and securely.

5
Managing Files Efficiently

In *Chapter 3, Creating Content for Effective Communication*, we saw how to create files. In this chapter, we will learn how to store them in a secure and efficient way.

Whether it was 10 minutes or 4 hours, you *did* spend part of your precious life creating and editing those files. Every file is like your baby, the fruits of your labor, output, a product, an asset. That is why it makes sense to store them with care.

The goal is to manage storage as well as collaboration without creating copies and wasting time on copy-paste.

We will cover these main topics in the chapter:

- Why storing just on the local drive is inefficient
- Why sending attachments is inefficient
- Why storing files on OneDrive is efficient
- Benefits of using OneDrive
- How to share files from OneDrive

Why storing files on the local drive is inefficient

Let's focus on the three most important reasons:

- **No backup**: Everyone knows that the local hard disk can fail. But we still do not end up taking regular backups. One hard disk malfunction can wipe off years of your work. Too much risk, isn't it?

- **Stuck to your PC (or device)**: You save a file on a laptop/PC/Mac and then switch it off. Now, you are in another place and you need the file. What can you do? Nothing. You cannot access your own file when you need it. Unfair, isn't it?

- **Copies**: This is the biggest enemy. Initially, it is just one file. But invariably, we need inputs from others. Now what? You send the file either as an email attachment or put it in a group chat. People edit the file and send it back. Congratulations! Now you have five copies! We waste a lot of time copy-pasting it into the sixth copy. Is the job done? Not yet. Another round, then one more... after some 27 copies, the final version of the file is ready (hopefully)! Sound familiar? Sound efficient?

We can discuss more disadvantages. But you got the point, right? Now let's see why sending attachments is a bad idea.

Why sending attachments is bad

In general, sending attachments is inefficient and less secure. The same problems exist with a file posted in a group chat. Here are the problems:

- Once you send an attachment, you lose control. The recipients can do whatever they want with the file.

- When you receive the edited files back, you need to combine them into a single file – which is extra work for you (hands versus brain).

- Scrolling each file to find changes and then copy-pasting is also error-prone as you may miss some of the changes and not copy-paste them at all. Of course, you can use the **Compare** (if **Track Changes** is off) or **Combine** (if **Track Changes** is on) function in Word on each pair of documents. If there are many contributors, even this process becomes tedious.

- After multiple iterations with attachments, people do not know where the latest version is.

- If you try to protect files by using passwords, you need to share the passwords with recipients of email attachments. How many passwords are you going to remember?

- Once you send the file, you cannot undo it. You cannot give editing access for a limited period.

- The recipient of attachments could forward the files to someone else (including your competitor!) and you would never know.

- If you send a file and then notice a mistake, you must send another copy – confusing everyone in the process.

- If some hacker steals the file on the way, they could also open and misuse the file.

Really bad. Is it not? Let's find a solution.

OneDrive, Teams, and Stream

The primary problem (root cause) is sending files to people, which leads to more copies. So why not keep the file in one place and let people come to edit it? Yes, we are also concerned about what happens if two people edit the file at the same time. Do not worry. All this has an easy and secure solution.

Each *one* of us needs *one* place to store our files in such a way that there is always *one* copy. Great. That is why the solution is called OneDrive for Business. When you store a file on OneDrive, only *one* person can see it – you.

The business version of OneDrive has comprehensive security and compliance features to protect your data from unauthorized use or hacking.

Files come in three types. Depending upon the type, we choose the ideal place for storage.

What kind of file?	Ideal place to store
Files that you create, control, and manage. On-demand needs to involve others.	OneDrive for Business
Files you created for a project or team activity. Everyone in the team/department should have access to it.	Microsoft Teams
Videos of any kind.	Microsoft Stream

In this chapter, we will focus on files of types 1 and 3. We will learn why OneDrive is the best place for your files and all the advantages plus security you get as a result.

We will cover Microsoft Teams in *Chapter 7, Efficient Teamwork and Meetings*.

> **Side Note**
>
> There are many other places to store files on the cloud, such as Google Drive, Dropbox, Box, and many others. Why are we talking only about OneDrive? Simple. Because most of the files we are creating are Microsoft Office files. Microsoft created Office as well as OneDrive (and Teams). That is why the integration between them is top class – unmatched by all other contenders. In addition, your login (authentication) happens on the Microsoft platform. Therefore, from the security point of view, you need to remember just one username and password.

Let's explore how storing files securely on the cloud can improve efficiency.

From now on, OneDrive refers to OneDrive for Business.

Using OneDrive on Windows 10

Let's get familiar with OneDrive and start using it – at least for new files you create. We will also handle common concerns and objections to using cloud storage in general. Most of the things mentioned here are equally applicable to OneDrive on Mac as well.

Do I have OneDrive?

If you have Windows 10, OneDrive should already be installed. If not, install it. OneDrive for Business uses a blue icon. Personal OneDrive uses a gray icon.

Figure 5.1 – OneDrive for Business icon

The latest version of OneDrive

It is important to make sure you have the latest version of OneDrive. Right-click the OneDrive icon in the System Tray and choose **Help and Settings | Settings | About**. Note the version displayed on your screen. In the following screenshot, I have blurred the version number to avoid confusion. Note down your version number.

About Microsoft OneDrive

☑ Get OneDrive Insider preview updates before release

Version ▓▓▓▓▓▓▓▓▓▓▓▓▓▓▓▓▓▓▓▓▓▓

© 2021 Microsoft Corporation. All rights reserved.

Figure 5.2 – OneDrive version

Next, use the link `https://support.microsoft.com/en-us/office/onedrive-release-notes-845dcf18-f921-435e-bf28-4e24b95e5fc0` to find the latest version of OneDrive. If your OneDrive version is older, download and install the new one. If required, talk to your IT team to help you.

Synchronizing files to the local drive

Usually, OneDrive files on the cloud synchronize automatically with the local drive. Make sure that your OneDrive is connected to the cloud. Right-click the OneDrive for Business icon (the blue icon) in the System Tray and choose **Help and Settings | Settings | Account**. You should see the Microsoft 365 ID as shown here.

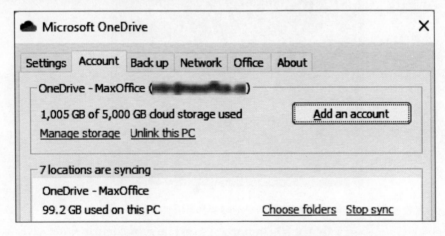

Figure 5.3 – OneDrive for Business account information

If you do not see an account, sign in using your Microsoft 365 ID and establish synchronization between OneDrive on the cloud and your PC. If required, ask your IT team to help you.

Right-click on the blue OneDrive icon and choose **Open your OneDrive <company name> folder**. This will open the local folder that is synced with OneDrive on the cloud.

Storing new files on OneDrive

You already have files on your local drive. We will talk about them later. Let's focus on the new files (Microsoft Office or other files) that you are going to create from now on.

Create your own sample file, say in Word, Excel, or PowerPoint, and save it on OneDrive. Do this on the PC. That way you can learn the benefits of using OneDrive during our journey in this chapter.

The first step is to save the file to OneDrive: **File | Save | OneDrive (company name)**. The business version of OneDrive shows the company name, the personal version does not. In either case, the related email ID is also visible. Let's say you saved the file as `sample.docx` in the OneDrive main folder (root folder).

Figure 5.4 – Save to OneDrive

Like with your `Documents` folder, it is important to create subfolders in OneDrive. Most of us have a familiar way of creating folders based upon work patterns. Continue the same pattern with OneDrive as well.

Now, where is the file stored? OneDrive. Where is OneDrive? On the cloud. So where is the file now? On the cloud. Right? Well, partially right. Let's see why.

Saving files on the local drive plus the cloud

As soon as you save the file to OneDrive, go to Windows File Explorer (*Windows + E*) and look for the **OneDrive (company name)** folder. You will see the file there on your local drive.

Figure 5.5 – OneDrive on the local disk

I just told you *not* to save files on the local drive. But OneDrive seems to have saved it to the local drive anyway. What is the point?

Well, the point is that this is not just a local file. Look at the icon – it shows that the file is synchronizing itself with OneDrive on the cloud.

Automatic backup and restore

If the local drive fails, you will not lose all your files. Just replace the hard disk and log in using the same M365 ID. That way, all the OneDrive files will synchronize automatically with the local drive.

Basically, storing the file on OneDrive is like having an automatic backup and restore system in place – less effort, more benefits.

Who can see my OneDrive files?

By default, only one person – you – can see files on your OneDrive. If you need input from others, you can share the file with others. Of course, you can stop sharing at any time.

In case you are wondering, nobody from Microsoft's data center can see your files.

Remember that this is OneDrive for Business. That is why the IT admin of your company manages OneDrive for all staff members. From a governance point of view, when a person leaves the company, the IT team can reassign their OneDrive to their manager or the new person who joins. The compliance team can also access OneDrive data for regulatory or legal needs. Read the article at https://efficiency365.com/2020/08/12/who-can-see-my-onedrive-files/ for details.

OneDrive file icons

Windows File Explorer shows small icons next to files (and folders) in the OneDrive folder. These icons indicate where the file is. Cloud icon files do not occupy any space on your local drive but are still searchable. You can also see their thumbnails. The person icon shows that the file or folder is shared.

Figure 5.6 – OneDrive file icons

When you double-click a cloud icon file, it will download if you are connected to the internet. Once it downloads, the icon will change to a green check mark.

If you want a file (or folder) to be always available on the device, right-click on it and choose **Always keep on this device**. This type of file shows a white check mark on a green background.

Editing files when offline

OneDrive is on the cloud. But to edit a local file with a check mark, you do not need an internet connection. You can edit the file while offline. Later, when you get an internet connection, the file will synchronize itself.

What if you edit offline from two devices? No problem. The changes will merge into the main file.

Deleting files

It is important to note that when you delete a file (or folder) from OneDrive, it will be removed from all devices. In case you delete a file by mistake, OneDrive has its own recycle bin.

Right-click on the blue OneDrive icon and choose **View online**. Now the OneDrive page will open in a browser. Choose **Recycle bin**. Select the file and choose **Restore**.

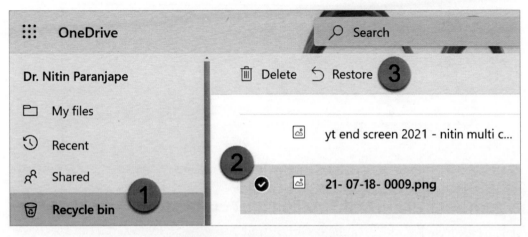

Figure 5.7 – OneDrive recycle bin

Files available across devices

From now on, OneDrive will manage the file synchronize across all your devices.

At this point, if you open the OneDrive app on mobile, you can see and edit the file there.

Even if you do not have your mobile and your original PC, you can go to any device with a browser and internet connection to see and edit this file. Go to Office.com on any browser, log in using your Office 365 ID, and go to OneDrive. You will find the file there as well. That's it.

OneDrive capacity

As of September 2021, you get 2 GB to 5 TB of space, based upon the type of Microsoft 365 license. This way, OneDrive becomes your main storage for all files. To check the available space, go to your PC and right-click on the OneDrive icon in the System Tray.

Choose **Help and Settings | Settings**. In the dialog, choose the **Account** tab. At the top, you will see the available and used space.

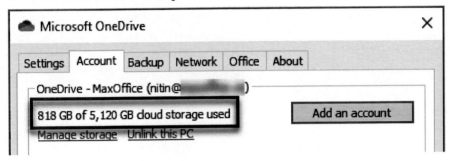

Figure 5.8 – OneDrive storage status

Documents and Desktop folder redirection

If you already have lots of files in the Desktop and Documents folders, you can ask OneDrive to upload and manage these files. This way, you do not have to manually move files and folders to the OneDrive folder on your PC; OneDrive assimilates them automatically. That way, you can work in your familiar folder environment while getting all the additional benefits of using OneDrive.

This is also known as **important PC folder integration**. Request corporate IT to enable it for you. If you have the permission, try to enable it yourself.

Go to the OneDrive icon in the System Tray, right-click, then go to **Help and Settings | Settings | Back up**. Follow the instructions to integrate the Desktop, Documents, and Pictures folders with OneDrive.

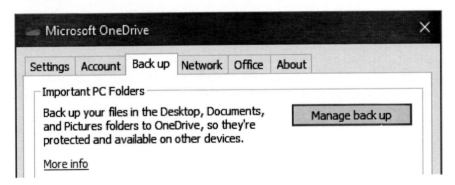

Figure 5.9 – Important PC folders

Benefits of storing files on OneDrive

In this section, we will cover the instant advantages you get by storing files on OneDrive. Other than saving to OneDrive, there is no extra effort involved.

AutoSave – no more file corruption

Often, while editing files, we forget to save. If the file hangs, we lose some of the changes. This will not happen when you start using OneDrive to store files. While you edit, OneDrive saves the file automatically. Always notice the **AutoSave** button and make sure it is on.

Figure 5.10 – AutoSave button

AutoSave drastically reduces the chances of file corruption and data loss.

Auto-versions – 500 versions (base file size counted quota)

No more **Save As** version 1, 2, 4, 5.32, and so on. OneDrive manages versions automatically. While you (and others) edit the file, versions save in the background. For each file, up to 500 versions are available. These versions are useful to view past changes and recover from mistakes.

If the file is open in Word, Excel, or PowerPoint, open the dropdown next to the filename and choose **Version History**.

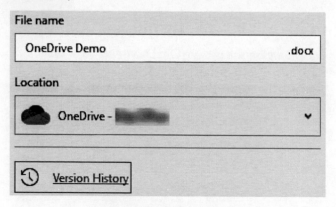

Figure 5.11 – Version History

You can also see the version history from the overflow menu next to the filename on the mobile and browser version of OneDrive.

Figure 5.12 – Version history

You can open a past version and restore it as the current version if required. Only the owner of the file can see the past versions. If you share the file with others, they can see only the latest version.

Editing in the browser/on mobile

Open the sample.docx file on the mobile OneDrive app. Now what happens? It will open even if you do not have Word installed. But to edit, you need the Word mobile app (or the Office mobile app). The file will synchronize automatically with the OneDrive cloud and other devices.

Ransomware protection

Ransomware attacks are increasing. Ransomware is a kind of virus that jumbles up (encrypts) your files. Files become unreadable. Then the hackers demand money (a ransom) to make your files usable. A local file change means the OneDrive (cloud) version of the file also will change – due to syncing.

In short, both the local copy and the OneDrive copy will now be unreadable. What is the solution? Pay the ransom to decrypt the files? Not at all. There is no need to pay a ransom for this attack.

Remember automatic versions? When ransomware affected the files, OneDrive saved the earlier version. You can restore that and get your data back.

The problem is that you may have thousands of files on OneDrive. Do you have to go to each file manually and restore the earlier version? Obviously not – even this thought is inefficient!

Go to OneDrive on the browser and click the sprocket in the top-right corner. Choose **Restore your OneDrive**.

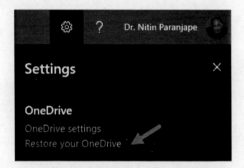

Figure 5.13 – Restore OneDrive

Now choose the day before the ransomware attack and OneDrive will do the rest. It will restore the earlier version of all files. That way, you can recover from a ransomware attack without paying a ransom.

For IT

If you have Microsoft threat protection integrated into Microsoft 365 E5, the process of detecting a ransomware attack, and OneDrive restoration are completely automated.

We have learned how to store and manage files efficiently. From now on, we do not want to send the file to others – let others come to the file to view or edit it. Let's learn the file-sharing benefits of OneDrive storage.

Sharing links from OneDrive

This is the most important benefit of storing files on OneDrive. Usually, we save a file, go to email, attach the file, and then send it. From now on, you can do better.
Send a link instead of the whole file – let people come to the file.

Word, Excel, and PowerPoint sharing

Use the **Share** button to send links to people. Click the **Share** button in the top-right corner in Word, Excel, and PowerPoint. If the file is not yet saved, it will first prompt you to save it to OneDrive.

Figure 5.14 – The Share button

Now, you can control who can do what with the file and for how long.

Understanding the Share dialog

Initially, it may look confusing. But let me explain.

Click the **Anyone with the link can view** option to see other options (1).

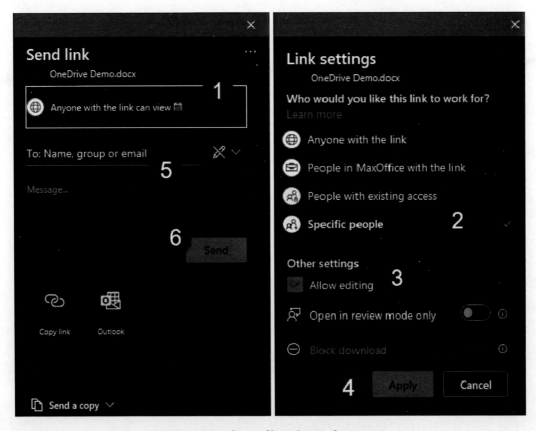

Figure 5.15 – Share a file with specific persons

The **Anyone with the link can view** option is an anonymous link. Anyone who can get hold of the link can open the file. When do you use this? For files that are meant for public visibility. For example, brochures, price lists, promotions, event invitations, e-books, white papers, user manuals, and so on.

For regular business document sharing, it is better to choose the **Specific people** option (labeled 2 in *Figure 5.15*). It is like sending an email to specific people from Outlook – but with a link instead of an attachment.

Allow editing

Now decide whether you want them to view the file or edit it (labeled 3 in *Figure 5.15*). If you want input from people, check the **Allow editing** checkbox.

Block download

If **Allow editing** is off, you can also **Block download**. People can open the file only in a browser. They can read it but cannot copy-paste or download it.

This is good for read-only content such as price lists, policies, product specifications, user manuals, and so on.

Adding email IDs

After you decide whether to allow editing and downloading, click on the **Apply** button (labeled 4 in *Figure 5.15*). Now it is time to add the email IDs of people you want to share the file with (5).

Also, add some explanatory text in the **Message...** area.

Sending the link

Finally, click the **Send** button to send the mail with the file link in it (labeled 6 in *Figure 5.15*). That is all there is to it.

We have selected the **Specific people** option. That is why this link will work *only* for those people. Other people cannot open the link. Therefore, it is more secure to share links instead of sending attachments.

Sharing with external people

You can share file links with dealers, distributors, suppliers, vendors, and customers. Any email IDs, including personal IDs such as Gmail, Yahoo, Apple, Hotmail, and so on will work. If this option is not available, request your IT team to look at the *Why sending links is safer* section later in this chapter.

External recipients do not need a Microsoft subscription. They do not need to have Word, Excel, or PowerPoint installed. They just need a browser and an internet connection to open and edit the file link that you have shared.

Even large files open quickly because the whole file does not need to download. Using OneDrive for Business, we can share files that are as large as 250 GB in size.

For added security, when an external person clicks the link, they must enter their email address again. Then they will receive a separate mail with a verification code. Once they type the code, the file link will open.

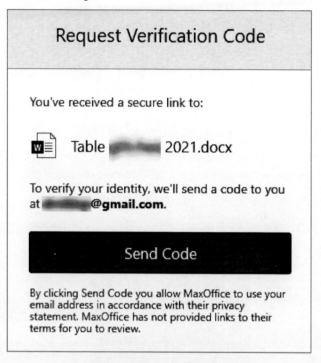

Figure 5.16 – Valid email verification code

That is why sharing links with external parties is more secure than sending attachments.

Initially, people may resist this way of sharing. But when you explain all the benefits to them, you will be able to convince them to use link sharing as the preferred method.

Sharing large files – up to 250 GB

Want to share large files? No problem. You can upload very large files to OneDrive. A single file can be 250 GB in size. Check the latest documentation (https://support.microsoft.com/en-us/office/restrictions-and-limitations-in-onedrive-and-sharepoint-64883a5d-228e-48f5-b3d2-eb39e07630fa) to find out the file size limit. Use this for sharing large video files, artwork, photos, illustrations, engineering drawings, logs, and so on.

Usually, when we share large files, people want to download the file and use it. Therefore, remember not to use the **Block download** option.

How to stop sharing

How will you remember which file you have shared with whom?

You do not need to. Click the **Share** button, click on the three dots – the overflow menu – and click **Manage Access** or open the **Shared with** section. Now you can see all the details of sharing.

You can stop sharing at any time or change from **Edit** to **View only**. In short, unlike with attachments, you are always in control.

File Explorer, web, and mobile sharing

If the document is not open in Word, Excel, or PowerPoint, you do not need to open it just to share the link. The same sharing dialog is available in three other places.

In Windows File Explorer, find the file, right-click, and choose **Share**.

With the mobile OneDrive app, click the overflow menu next to the filename and choose **Share**.

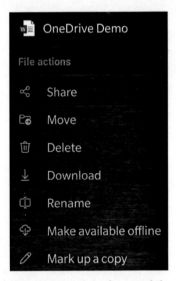

Figure 5.17 – Share from mobile

In the browser, the share button is right next to the filename.

Figure 5.18 – Share from the browser

Forwarded links will not work

When the other person opens the link, a message shows that this is a direct link.

Figure 5.19 – Direct links are safer

If this person forwards the mail to another person, the link will not work – another security benefit of sharing links instead of attachments. What is more, you can see the file details with a log of who opened the file and when!

Figure 5.20 – OneDrive file activity

Share contextually with @mention in comments

Sometimes, we want others to look at a specific area of the file and get their input or approval. It could be one paragraph in Word, a specific PivotTable in Excel, or a particular slide in PowerPoint.

In this example, we will use a paragraph in Word. Let's say we want the boss to look at the cost of the project and then approve it.

Select the desired area – in this case, the cost – right-click, and choose **New Comment**. Type the text and then type the person's name starting with the @ sign. This is like @ mentions we use in social media.

Figure 5.21 – Share with @mention

When your boss opens the email, the paragraph you highlighted is right there. Your boss can click the **Add Comment** button to enter comments directly in the email.

The comments will merge with the original comment automatically.

This way, you can share a part of the document in a contextual manner for precise and efficient collaboration.

Editing together

So far, we have shared the link with others. There is still only one copy of the file. People can open and edit the file. The changes go to the same file.

What if multiple persons try to edit the same file at the same time? No problem at all. It works amazingly well.

Each person can continue editing while others are also editing. Word temporarily locks the paragraph you are editing so that others cannot edit it. When you move to another paragraph, Word unlocks it. This is a simple and effective way to work together without confusion.

In the case of Excel and PowerPoint, if two people are editing at the same item, the last person to do the edit wins. There is no locking.

Figure 5.22 – Multiple persons can edit the same document

There is no limit to the number of people who can edit at the same time. This means you will never have to struggle with multiple copies of the document – no more repetitive copy-paste. Each person can use a different device. Editing together (coauthoring is the technical name) works with desktop apps, browser apps, and mobile apps for Word, Excel, and PowerPoint (and the combined Office mobile app).

The best way to learn about this feature is to try it yourself with your colleague(s). In the meantime, watch this video demonstration. Learn how to edit Word, Excel, and PowerPoint files together – with a live demo.

https://hi.switchy.io/etg

The latest version is always visible

Have you ever sent a mail with an attachment and then realized that there was a mistake in the file? You try to recall the mail – sometimes it works, sometimes it does not. You then send another mail with the corrected file. Some people read the wrong file.

When you share files as links, this will never happen. Why? Because we are sending a link. You correct or change the file – no problem. The link does not change. People who click on the link will always see the latest (and correct) version. Problem solved!

Why sending links is safer

Often, external sharing is disabled for security reasons. However, compared to sending files as attachments, sending links is safer and more efficient. These are the benefits of sharing files as links:

- A file never leaves the organization.
- Extra OTPs for email ownership checks.
- You can block downloading, copying, and printing.
- The latest version is always available.
- You can stop sharing at any time.
- There's an audit trail of who saw the file and when.

Therefore, you should encourage everyone to share links as much as possible.

Does it mean that you will never need to send attachments? No.

There may be legal or statutory requirements where you must send an attachment. Here are some examples: a payslip, an offer letter, a legal notice, a request for a proposal, a resignation letter, an invoice, and so on.

For these cases, you must send attachments as expected. In all other cases, use links.

If you are concerned about data loss prevention, use Microsoft DLP – it integrates seamlessly with OneDrive, Teams, SharePoint, Exchange, and on-premises data sources.

Non-Microsoft files

OneDrive is a drive for storing files. You can save all types of files to it, for example, text files, AutoCAD, CoralDRAW, Adobe Photoshop, images, and so on.

Of course, some dangerous types of files such as executables and script files are blocked for security reasons. But, as a business user, we do not create those types of files anyway. Files with macros can be stored on OneDrive.

A single file on OneDrive could be up to 250 GB in size. That is why, next time you want to share a large file, just use OneDrive – there's no need to look for some random (and potentially unsafe) cloud storage providers. Check the latest documentation – `https://support.microsoft.com/en-us/office/restrictions-and-limitations-in-onedrive-and-sharepoint-64883a5d-228e-48f5-b3d2-eb39e07630fa` – to find out the file size limit.

OneDrive can show a thumbnail view of the file contents even if you do not have the actual software installed. Here is an example.

Figure 5.23 – OneDrive thumbnails

How can you share the files? Go to File Explorer or a mobile app or browser and click the **Share** button. The options are the same as what we saw earlier.

The recipient of the shared link needs to have the relevant software at their end. For example, if you send a `.psd` file to someone, they need to have Adobe Photoshop to edit it.

Who edited what?

Editing is done in the relevant app, such as Word, Excel, or PowerPoint – not by OneDrive. Therefore, OneDrive itself cannot keep track of what happened inside each file. But Word, Excel, and PowerPoint do provide this facility.

With Word, you can enable **Track Changes** to know who changed what.

With Excel, you can right-click on any cell or range and choose **Show Changes**.

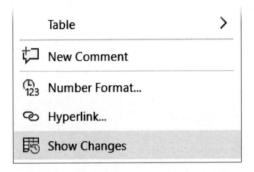

Figure 5.24 – Who changed what in Excel

With PowerPoint, you will see colored borders around items edited by others along with their names.

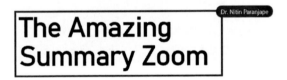

Figure 5.25 – Who edited what in PowerPoint

Files shared with me

Someone sent you a link 1 month back by email. You want to open the file now. Do you need to find that email? Not at all. If it is a Word, Excel, or PowerPoint file, just open the app and choose **File | Open | Shared with me**. All the files should be there.

OneDrive on the web also has a separate area for files **Shared with you** (2) and files **Shared by you** (3):

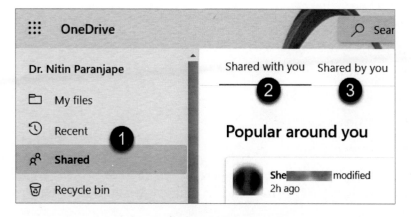

Figure 5.26 – Shared files in OneDrive

OneDrive benefits summary

Let's summarize the benefits of storing files on OneDrive. Sharing happens with others. Therefore, others also need to know the benefits of using OneDrive. When you start sending links instead of attachments, assume that the other parties may not know the benefits. It is important to educate them. Otherwise, they will compel you to send attachments!

Here are the benefits of using OneDrive:

- Automatic saving.
- Automatic backup.
- Automatic versioning.
- Ransomware protection.
- You can rename/move a file while open.
- You can edit on any device or browser.
- You can edit offline and synchronize.
- You can edit the same file together.
- It eliminates repeated cutting and pasting.
- Controlled sharing – view/edit/block download.
- Send links to external people.
- External link security with OTP.

- Share large files up to 250 GB.

- Manage non-Office files.

- Contextual sharing with @mention.

- Forwarded links do not work.

- The latest version is always visible.

- Personal view in Excel.

In short, you can create better-quality documents faster. But there is more. We will explore another benefit of using OneDrive in *Chapter 7, Efficient Teamwork and Meetings*.

Summary

In this chapter, we have covered the advantages of using OneDrive over the local drive for storing our files. You have got a clear idea of why sending attachments should be avoided for safety and enhanced productivity. You can now implement your knowledge to efficiently manage your files using the functionalities of OneDrive and make the best out of this wonderful application.

Now it is time to manage time! In *Chapter 6, Time and Task Management*, we will learn how to streamline our pending work, delegate tasks, and find time to do the work.